HUGH COMPTON WARNER

Hugh Compton Warner.

HUGH COMPTON WARNER

The Story of a Vocation

BY

NANCY LE PLASTRIER WARNER

> . . . but priests
> Should study passion; how else cure mankind
> Who come for help in passionate extremes?
> Robert Browning

LONDON

S·P·C·K

1958

First published in 1958
by S.P.C.K.
Holy Trinity Church, Marylebone Road,
*London, N.W.*1
Printed in Great Britain by
Billing and Sons, Ltd., Guildford and London

© Nancy le Plastrier Warner 1958

To his family whom he loved,
To the families that he helped,
To God's Family which he served.

AUTHOR'S NOTE

My thanks are due in the first place to the Bishop of St Albans and Miss Ena Steel who simultaneously, though independently, asked me to try to write my husband's life, and who have consistently helped, criticized, and encouraged me in the task. Without them it would not have been begun.

Next I have to thank Miss E. M. Jeal for much help over the Epsom chapter, Mrs Noel Paton for useful criticism and friendly blue-pencil, and Dr A. R. Winnett for encouragement and advice. For permission to quote from *Christian Youth Leadership in Clubs and Youth Centres* by Hugh Warner I am indebted to the S.C.M. Press Ltd.; and to the Editor of the *Guildford Diocesan Leaflet,* Canon K. D. Evans, I am grateful for permission to quote from the *Guildford Diocesan Gazette.* To the many friends, relations, and ex-parishioners whose words or letters I have, whether with or without permission, so freely quoted, I can only say that without them the book could hardly have taken shape.

To Mrs Mercer, my husband's secretary at Church House, my debt is incalculable. She has typed and re-typed my constantly emended MS. as a sheer labour of love in her free time, amidst pressure of work at the Moral Welfare Office. Without her the book would certainly never have been published.

NANCY LE P. WARNER

Dorking,
December 1957.

CONTENTS

LIST OF ILLUSTRATIONS

PROLOGUE

"What then shall we do? Where shall we find a character
at once gentle and high-spirited? For I suppose a gentle
nature is the opposite of a spirited one?"

"Apparently it is."

"Nevertheless a man who is devoid of either gentleness or
spirit cannot possibly make a good guardian."

Plato : *Republic*

"SINCE we get half our genes from each parent, it is easy
to see why we have a little bit of father and a little bit
of mother in us," wrote Hugh Warner in his booklet
for teen-agers, *Science and You, an Account of Human
Reproduction and Personal Relationship*. Seldom can there
have been a more sharply contrasted couple than his own
parents-to-be when they met on the P. & O. liner *Norman,*
bound for South Africa at the beginning of this century. His
father, also Hugh Warner, a quiet, delicate accountant of
thirty-three, with a Quaker background and temperament,
and a certain dry humour, had been sent out as a young man
to a warm climate for his health. He was returning now
from furlough to his bank in Umtali in Southern Rhodesia.
Despite his weak lungs he had a fine tenor voice and was
much in request for ship's concerts, at which he was accompanied *con fuoco* by Winifred Wright, an energetic young
whirlwind of twenty with a strong Edinburgh accent, a
glorious crown of hair, and the extravert nature of a born
reformer, who was going out to keep house for her brother,
Dr Robert Wright, in Port Elizabeth.

All her life any kind of need or sickness proved an irre-
sistible challenge to Winnie's tender heart and Scots readi-

ness to "take charge". When she arrived in South Africa she had made up her mind that what the delicate young man on the boat needed was a good wife. He, for his part, was equally convinced that he had found one. But Dr Wright steadily opposed the engagement. A delicate man thirteen years older than herself was not, in his judgement, a good risk for his young sister. Nevertheless, he had the highest regard for Mr Warner, a lovable man of great integrity who has been well described by his younger daughter: "He was a great Christian, and a great churchman. I shall never forget going up to his dressing-room one morning to tell him breakfast was ready—burst in and found him kneeling by his bed saying his prayers. It made a very profound impression on me, as I crept out. Two things I often remember about him. One, that he made it a rule which he expected us to follow—though only by example—that church was attended at least once on a Sunday, *every* Sunday. Two, that he told me once that he tried to make it a rule that he NEVER lost his temper. He did it in admiration of a manager he had who never lost his. How well he kept that rule!" On this occasion he both kept his temper and gained his point. No opposition could withstand his quiet tenacity and Winnie's spirited determination, and eventually after seven months, on 12 November 1902, they were married. The following year, on 31 August, their first baby was born, and named Hugh Compton, after his father and grandfather.

He inherited the salient characteristics of both parents in full measure, his mother's fearless "drive" and enthusiasm, his father's peaceable patience; and the contrasting tendencies seemed to complement and balance each other, blending into a harmonious whole. His enthusiasm was dynamic but controlled and reasoned; his tolerance and patience were positive and creative, never a negative "peace at any price".

While his exceptional energy in parish life was proverbial, yet a Quaker lady who often attended his church in Epsom remarked: "I could have told the Vicar came of Friends stock: he is so calm and unhurried."

A striking instance of this curious contrast was the occasion in Epsom when he arrived home one morning about eleven o'clock after a staff meeting exclaiming, "I've just discovered I'm supposed to be speaking in Lancashire this afternoon: I thought it was next week!" There was a train leaving in ten minutes' time (he could catch it if he ran) which landed him in Bolton with only just time enough to get to the meeting. He made his appearance, calm, smiling, unperturbed, with one minute to spare, completely devoid of fuss, rush or agitation, and the audience never suspected, listening to him, that they had nearly neither speech nor speaker!

These things happened, undoubtedly, because his engagement book was always overfull. He could never refuse a request, and tried to fit a quart into a pint pot all his life. What saved the situation was his capacity to concentrate on one thing at a time and to dismiss from his mind everything but what he was doing at the moment, whether it was writing an article or playing a game with the children. As in church he was unhurried, so in visiting he was never seen to glance at clock or watch, or seem conscious that he had anything on his mind save the people he was with. He gave his whole attention to an interview, even though another engagement was waiting in a quarter of an hour's time. That would demand the same total absorption when it came. "What *peace* he brings with him," said a young man whom he visited on a sick-bed, shortly before his own last illness, "as if he has all the time there is simply for *you*."

For his activity was deliberate: it was not mere restlessness. He just could not help being aware of needs wherever

3

he met them; people that needed help, evils that needed tackling, opportunities that needed to be seized, untouched areas of parish or civic life that needed to be won for God. "There's another job that will have to be done by someone," he said once; "I suppose it will be me!" But his calm was equally deliberate; it was not mere English phlegm. "Mere annoyance and temper and futile seeking for sympathy or bewailing of this mishap is no help at all," he wrote once of a disappointment. "The silence of prayer is the only thing sure enough to fall back upon."

"The silence of prayer" was the underlying truth of all the activity : a kind of stillness at the heart of the whirlpool. . . . "Sorry for this short scrappy letter and desperate hurry," he wrote in his busy Student Christian Movement days. "Are you having a nice restful and refreshing time? I am, really—in spite of the seeming rush—(somewhere *underneath,* you know)." It was characteristic that his favourite prayer was the Collect from Compline, which asks that "we who are wearied by the changes and chances of this fleeting world may repose upon Thy eternal changelessness".

We do not choose what qualities we inherit, but we choose which we will cultivate. Hugh knew which traits he most admired in his father's and his mother's families, and he sought to develop them in himself and in his children. His favourite story of Warner presence of mind and self-control was of his Aunt Hilda, who, going up to the nursery one day, had discovered her tiny son standing on the window-sill *outside* the window. Not so much as a gasp escaped her. Without his noticing that she had come or gone, she stole from the room, ran downstairs and rang the dinner gong. A few minutes later the small boy[1] appeared safely in the dining-room.

[1] Now headmaster of the Pilgrim School, Winchester.

4

In his mother Hugh especially admired the undaunted manner in which, regardless of obstacles, she would find some practical way of helping those who aroused her sympathy. Almost single-handed, against conventional white opinion, she fought to establish a district nurse for the native population of George, in Cape Colony; opening a District Nurses' Fund in her husband's bank, persuading the Bishop to head it with a generous subscription, giving piano lessons to swell it, and talking the Town Council into contributing £50.

If "Blessed are the peacemakers" was the spontaneous epitaph of all friends and relations for Hugh's father, his mother might more truly earn Thucydides' immortal tribute to the Athenians, "Born to give neither themselves nor anyone else any peace!"

From his mother, too, he inherited that histrionic sense which has carried more than one member of the family on to the stage, and which caused Felton Rapley, his organist in Epsom, to remark once after a festival service, "You and I, if I may say so, sir, have a sense of the dramatic!" "A born impresario," his mother-in-law called him; and Dr Gilbert Russell wrote of him, "He was not the man to despise an effective piece of showmanship; and he was blessed with the sort of simplicity that does not always go with it"—again underlining the surprising balance of opposites. For though some things in his ordering of Church services might illustrate his *sens de theatre*—the fanfare of chords ushering in the Creed, "the battle-cry of Christendom"; or the singing of a hymn from the steps outside the church on the early morning of Ascension Day—there was nothing "theatrical" about his own behaviour, which was only conspicuous by its dignity and restraint. Surely no one ever kept more still, or displayed fewer mannerisms, in the pulpit.

He was not, in the accepted sense, a great preacher, in spite of charm and conviction. He wanted always to say too much, and his sermons, some said, "sagged in the middle". In a life lived at his pace he gave too little time to their detailed construction and polish. To the details of services, on the other hand, he paid great attention. His use of silence (and when Hugh, with his Quaker blood, said, "Let us pray in silence," it was no perfunctory pause), his sense of timing, his beautifully modulated voice which could overcome the worst acoustics, his sensitiveness to the little things that "put people off", above all, his own innate capacity for wonder, all contributed to an atmosphere in which the congregation could worship God in Spirit and in Truth.

"Wonder," he said in a sermon broadcast from St Martin's, Epsom, "is at the root of joy; and joy is at the heart of love . . . About GOD there is much that I do not understand, but a great deal that fills me with wonder." It was in his celebration of the Holy Communion that he especially expressed, and awoke in others, his own sense of the numinous. "O worship the Lord in the beauty of holiness: let the whole earth stand in awe of Him" was his favourite opening sentence for Mattins or Evensong. It was the keynote of every celebration. In a church full of coughs and rustles he could create an almost tangible stillness by the way he said the Prayer of Consecration. One could feel it winning the battle against fidgets of mind or body, carrying harassed souls out of this over-busy, noisy, distracted world to the region where there is "silence in heaven for the space of half an hour".

Not only in his own church and congregation, but wherever he took occasional duty, people remarked on this power to kindle true devotion. "I think," one wrote, "it was the way he made one feel his great love for Our Lord." Indeed, Hugh loved God with all his heart, even from boy-hood days; with all his mind, as his letters from Oxford and Westcott House will show; with all his soul, as his own churchpeople knew; and to the end with all his strength. And his neighbour? "Mostly we remember him for personal reasons," wrote the Vicar of Dorking in the *Guildford Diocesan Gazette,* "his insight and, in the Quaker sense, his concern. He would let himself become involved in the needs of people, and would take trouble pastorally with those whom others might prudentially call hopeless."

His tolerance and good temper on committees was re-markable. One of his colleagues on the Moral Welfare Council has described it: "I used to wonder however he managed to do all the amount of work he got through and still look fresh and calm and always cheerful. If things did not go the way he wanted or had hoped, he never got 'ratty' or aggressive (as *I* do), but always kept pleasant and was unfailingly courteous." "Such a very *courteous* man!" was the comment of a Sister who nursed him in his last illness. What is courtesy, after all, but the practice of charity? If at times he failed to see another's point of view, that was a failure of head, not of heart; for though quick of insight and imagination, his reasoning processes were slow and he could be curiously obtuse. But though sometimes impervious to an objection, he was never impatient with the objector.

In his file was found, after his death, a set of notes for a Quiet Day—no date or occasion is recorded, but the scheme of one address indicates that it was for the members of some committee:

"Charity suffereth long (I can't stand that fellow) and is
          kind (That's the secretary's fault),
   Charity envieth not (Some people have been on too long),

7

Charity vaunteth not itself (Wait till they elect me secretary),
   is not puffed up (Of course, I've been on this committee
      longer than most),
   doth not behave itself unseemly (!),
   seeketh not her own (I don't see what I'm going to get
      out of this),
   is not easily provoked (I'll resign),
   thinketh no evil (What was he hinting at?),
   rejoiceth not in iniquity (Didn't I say he'd make a mess
      of it?),
   believeth all things (Be careful—can't trust a word he
      says),
   hopeth all things (It'll be a failure, no one will come),
   endureth all things (The perfect chairman)."

"He really likes people, doesn't he?" someone remarked
after his first Parochial Church Council meeting at Bishopthorpe; and so he did—all sorts of people . . . including
"awkward" ones. The conventionally virtuous were sometimes shocked at the types who engaged his sympathies. But
Hugh never classed people as "types" or saw them, even in
his marriage guidance work, as "cases". They were always
people "who just need loving", as he was fond of saying.

Children and young people quickly felt at home with him.
Shyness or nervousness dissolved before that radiant smile.
He would often make for a railway carriage where he had
spotted toddlers or infants in arms, and would probably
spend the journey reading to or playing with the restless
ones. He was the moving joyous spirit of any party, whether
"shouting out the battle-cry of freedom" in shorts and open-
neck shirt round a camp fire; or presiding at a harvest supper
clad in a farmer's smock, red neckerchief and outrageous
wig; or swathed in cotton-wool and red cloak, apologizing

8

in a thin, quavering voice for being late for the family Christmas tree as a reindeer had sprained an ankle. And all alike would end up simply and naturally with thanksgiving to God for the joy of fun and laughter and fellowship. His life was all of a piece, and none knew it better than his own family, which most fully experienced what Love meant to Hugh Warner.

Love was his vocation—the demonstration in every part of life, through Christian worship, through parochial fellowship, through public life, through personal relations, of the love that never faileth, the true Charity of God. And of Charity, so he always maintained, not only the beginning but the inspiration and touchstone is the Home. It was in the sphere of home and family life that he was to make his greatest contribution to the Church; but whether in home, pulpit, youth club or committee, he was always essentially the same man, and no one has summed him up better than Kenneth Carey, Principal of Westcott House: "He was such a help to us all; so wise, so human, so good—and such fun."

PART I
PREPARATION

1

BEGINNING

Home, Schooldays

Happy those early days when I
Shin'd in my Angel-infancy! . . .
When on some gilded cloud, or flow'r
My gazing soul would dwell an hour,
And in those weaker glories spy
Some shadows of eternity.
Henry Vaughan

THE new baby slept peacefully in the house at Umtali,
while his mother played the piano with characteristic
energy, and the coloured servants barricaded their
quarters against lions rumoured to be in the neighbourhood.
All his life Hugh refused to be disturbed by external circumstances unless they were such as seriously to claim his attention; such, for instance, as the visit of Bishop Furse of
Pretoria, who, coming to Umtali in the course of a diocesan
visitation, called at the Warners' home and saw their seven-
months-old son. Twenty-six years later Hugh would meet
him again, to be accepted as an ordinand in his diocese of
St Albans.

When the baby was nine months old his father was pro-
moted to be manager of the bank in Mossel Bay, and the
family left Rhodesia for the coast of Cape Colony. That
coast nearly saw the end of him. Tom, the coloured nurse
"boy", though devoted to his charge, was not altogether
reliable, and one day was found dozing in the sun on the

beach while the baby crawled swiftly and enquiringly towards the breakers. Needless to say, it was his mother who swept on to the scene in the nick of time, rescued the baby and sacked the culprit. Soon afterwards a second boy, Cyril, was born, and within a year a third baby was on the way. Life was beginning to overwhelm Winnie Warner; the heat of Africa after her bracing Edinburgh, the native servants, the growing family. Her doctor ordered her home to have her baby in England. The little boys whom she brought with her were "adopted" for the time being by their father's sisters, Cyril going to a married aunt and Hugh to his aunts Ethel and Alice at Barclay's Bank in Hoddesdon, Hertfordshire, where they lived with their mother and their brother Clement, the manager. This was Hugh's first visit to "The Bank", which was to play a big part in his boyhood. There he was "Hughie", to distinguish him from his father, and his Aunt Ethel became his much-loved foster-mother. When the family had returned to South Africa, complete with the new sister, he "wrote" to her, dictating to his father, who has written in the margin, "All his own":

"MY DARLING SWEETHEART,

"I am coming back soon. How are my little flowers getting on. I have tea in the bedroom—I kind boy to Cyril. I had tea this afternoon down at Mrs Hoares, I was so good I had a red orange. Please give Grannie a kiss and a love and a hug and Uncle Clemmie. I coming soon. I wearing little trousers. I growing out of my clothes. A good hug to you and kiss.

"Your
"HUGHIE."

It was characteristic of him to ask after the "little flowers". Later on, as a schoolboy, he was to win a prize at Hoddesdon Flower Show for the best arranged vase. Love of nature and

of beauty in all its aspects was something very deep-rooted.
The aunt who had taken his mother's place in keeping
house for Dr Wright in Port Elizabeth remembers him, on
a family visit, taking her hand and saying, "Come and see
the sunset, Aunt Mabel." She loved sunsets too, but she
thought it rather remarkable in so small a boy. Writing
from Karlovsci, in his student days, he describes Yugo-
Slavia as "this land of sunsets", and his letters were always
"as full of scenery as a Walter Scott novel", as someone once
teased him.

"I wish sometimes," he wrote when about to visit his
fiancée's old home in Wales, "I could take you back to *my*
mountains, forests, burning endless karroo—the smell of
giant eucalyptus trees, the secret silence of virgin forest
streams. You would see what I loved almost more than anything, the vivid lights and trellised shadows on the water—
so dark sometimes that you held your breath, wondering
where the waters began and ended, and whether *anyone* had
ever been along those banks before—(I often used to wonder
this!). The brilliance of birds' wings and bodies caught in
the patches of sunlight, the heavy forest silence, which leaves
a sort of pain inside; the air shimmering with heat and the
wonderful music of winged insects which one hears sometimes in English woods on a summer afternoon, but never
with quite the same sense of mystery."

(One remembers with some amazement that he left South
Africa at six years old.)

When his father was moved to the Standard Bank in
George he was surrounded by "scenery", for his home was
within view of the lovely Outeniqua range of mountains and
within picnicking distance of the glorious Wilderness. By
this time the fourth baby, Maud, had arrived to make a
compact family of two boys and two girls. But four babies

under five years was a handful, with only the help of native servants, who distressed the housewife and the Presbyterian in their Scottish mistress when they secreted underdone beef under the mattress or received men visitors through their bedroom windows. Yet she had more true sympathy with the native population than the European, having little patience, in her downright unconventional nature, with the superficial tea-drinking, bridge-playing set-up of White society. Nor could she easily settle in her husband's church; and the climate was a constant drain. By the time Hughie was nearly seven years old she was on the verge of a breakdown, and was sent home again with all four children. The small Hugh watched her with compassion as on the boat she struggled with the searing pain in her head which was to dog her all her life. "You go and lie down, Mummy," he said. "*I'll* look after the little girls." And she went, while he walked up and down the deck with a little hand in each of his.

This time both boys went to the Bank at Hoddesdon, and when their mother was fit to travel again she was allowed to return to George alone. Later on the little girls were taken out by a friend, on the understanding that the boys should follow them when she had recovered her full strength. But when the time came the 1914 War had begun, and their father was very unwilling to allow them to sail. A friend who was returning to South Africa offered to bring them out with him, but mercifully their father still refused. The boat was mined and there were no survivors. After that it was agreed that the boys should stay and go to school in England, living with "Grannie", Uncle Clem and the aunts at the Bank, and from then onwards for them it was "home".

Warner relations were legion. In Aunt Ethel's generation

alone there were thirty-six cousins, all descended from one John Warner, the bell-founder, in whose foundry were cast the bells which chime the quarters of Big Ben.[1] In a complicated, prolific family tree all except Hugh's particular branch are Quakers. His grandfather, Compton Warner, had married a churchwoman, and the Bank family now attended church, either in Hoddesdon or in the neighbouring parish of Broxbourne, where Uncle Clem was scoutmaster and sang in the choir.

The two boys sang there with him, and there in due course they were prepared for Confirmation in a way which made a deep impression on Hugh. "Are you one of those to whom it's not a proper Confirmation without 'O Jesus, I have promised'?" Archbishop Temple once asked him when choosing the hymns for a Confirmation in Bishopthorpe. "Indeed I am!" replied Hugh. It was one of his favourite hymns, and he never sang it without recollecting his own Confirmation, which meant so much to him. It summed up that living relationship of personal obedience to "his Master and his Friend", which to him was the essence of Christianity.

His father wrote to him from South Africa:

"Well, Hugh, I was very pleased to hear that you had been Confirmed, although you are somewhat young still you appear to be a thoughtful boy for your age, and it certainly should be a help to you, especially when you have to go away to a boarding school, which I suppose you must before long. I always think of you, dear boy, on the first Sundays, that you will be going to Holy Communion. Life at present is not very hard to you, I do not suppose, but if you train

---

[1] The story of the original ill-fated Big Ben, cast by the Warner Brothers, is told in *The Book of Big Ben*, by Alfred Gilgrass, and an old *Punch* had some amusing verses about it.

yourself while you are young to do always what is best and honourable, you will find that life will become easier and it will become a second nature, as we call it, to do kind actions, to keep your temper when provoked, to keep yourself pure in mind and action. I often wish I could be with you and dear Cyril, so that I could have chats with you, about things you must guard against. The great thing to strive for is to lead clean, noble lives and to be true Christian men. Be *manly* in the truest possible sense, but *don't* be prigs. Example is the best thing, just quietly doing your duty and doing everything with your whole heart—and let everybody feel you can *always* be depended on, both in *word* and *deed*. Let it always be said at whatever school you are at or where you and Cyril may be, 'The Warner boys may have their faults, but you can always rely on them.' I don't know if I have expressed myself very well, but read this over carefully, both you and dear old Cyril—I hope you boys are pals; keep together and share each other's thoughts, troubles and pleasures and don't try to 'lord it' over each other—be helpful to one another."

Even so, in similar vein, had old Compton Warner been used to write to his sons. It is in the family, as Hugh would later stress when preparing couples for marriage, that values and standards are learned and passed on. Hugh's parents had not abdicated responsibility when they left him in England. His mother often wrote in the manner of her birthday letter when he was eleven: "Try to do something for dear Auntie Ethel, Grannie or Uncle Clem *every day*. It may only be a tiny thing, but if it is done kindly, from your heart, then it is counted as much perhaps as a very big thing. It is not what we *do*, remember, Hughie, but the doing it with a kind heart, that counts."

Some months before his Confirmation he had confided in

his Aunt Ethel that he wanted to be a clergyman when he grew up. Miss Thornton, an influential member of Broxbourne congregation, came to hear of this through his Aunt Alice, who worked under her at the Hertford Mission. She took a great interest in the boy and discovered that his teachers at St Catherine's School thought him promising. His headmaster had summed up his previous term's report, in which he had appeared first or second in his class in every subject, "This pupil is probably the most consistent and hardest-working boy in the school. His work is always reliable." Knowing that the family were hard pressed financially as a result of the various passages to and from South Africa, Miss Thornton and the vicar put their heads together and between them offered to pay the fees to send him to a good London school. There was no favouritism in the Warner family, and his father wrote: "Mother and I will be delighted, dear boy, for you to be a clergyman if you feel that way, it is certainly the finest profession that a man can take up—but you will have to work hard for it. I often pray God to guide both of you as to what is the best profession that you will be suited to, and you must do the same. It is *most* kind of Miss Thornton to suggest helping us to send you to a more advanced school, and I hope before long we shall be able to arrange it. I do hope though when you go, dear Cyril will be able to go with you. I should hate the idea of your being separated, and I expect you and he would too."

The school chosen for Hugh was the City of London School. Another kind friend came to Cyril's rescue and sent him to St Paul's, so the boys were at least able to travel up and down to London together each day. Their friendship, as their father had expressed the hope, was very close and true throughout their lives, and only strengthened by the fierce arguments they both enjoyed. "Goodness, *how* he could argue!" groans Cyril, when talking of those days. "No one could ever win an argument against Hugh!"

Undoubtedly the strongest formative influence on both brothers in their boyhood was their Uncle Clement, a smaller edition of their father, with the same spare Warner build, kindly humour and transparent goodness. From him they learned their love of the Scout movement and all that it stands for. Many were the summer camps to which he took the boys, and camping remained Hugh's favourite form of holiday all his life. "I just love," he once wrote, "sleeping out in the open; you can hear the secret whispers of uncut grass close to your ear, and there's a rather special kind of quiet." He was never happier than when initiating others, and in later years his own children, into the joys of "tracking" and woodlore.

His most memorable camp was that of July 1917, when, as a patrol leader of nearly fifteen, he took his patrol camping at Waltham Cross. It was the week-end of the first daylight air-raid over London, and ever afterwards the sound of enemy raiders conjured up the memory of lying prone in a deep ditch and the smell of silverside of salt beef simmering over a camp fire.

The other great influence on Hugh's growing mind was the Bible Class run by Mr Walker, the Vicar of Broxbourne. He had been a missionary in Uganda, and—even more exciting, perhaps, to a boy's mind—he had one glass eye, having lost an eye playing bows and arrows among the tombstones as a boy. From him Hugh learned a definitely evangelical churchmanship for which he was always thankful, even though he moved from it in later years.

Perhaps because all his strongest interests were at home, in choir, Scouts, rowing club, bird-nesting with Cyril—to say nothing of his pet canary, Joy, "who laid two eggs in one day and then died"—his London school never meant very much to Hugh. Moreover, the war had taken the cream of the teaching profession, and not all elderly stop-gaps were of the calibre of Mr Chips.

It was when he was sixteen and had reached the rank of sergeant in the school O.T.C. that his mother came back to England. The war was over and she could bear the parting from her sons no longer. A friend who was headmistress of a school in Maidenhead offered her the post of assistant matron. By taking this and giving piano lessons she was able to have all four children with her there for a year, and brothers and sisters were re-united. The boys continued going up to London daily, but money was still scarce, and Hugh writes to his father, "Cheer up, Dad! I am working at high pressure and am doing my very best to pay for myself through a scholarship." His mother, however, with all a Scot's ambition and seriousness about education, evidently did not think the pressure high enough and had grave doubts about the scholarship. One night, when boyish high spirits had been more to the fore than homework, she exclaimed in exasperation that he would *never* be a clergyman! Her friend the headmistress heard her and offered to write to someone she knew on the Central Committee for Training for the Ministry, and make enquiries about grants and possibilities. It was suggested that Hugh might test his vocation by going to the newly opened Ordination Test School at Knutsford. This was intended primarily for ex-Service men, but there were still a few places to spare, and Hugh, though much younger than the other candidates, was given one of them. Thus, in January 1922, at the age of seventeen, he began what he used afterwards to delight his Youth Fellowships by describing as "my time in jail".

2

GROWTH

Knutsford, Oxford

By religious experience we ought to mean an experience
which is religious through and through—an experiencing
of all things in the light of the knowledge of God. It is
this, and not any moment of illumination, of which we say
that it is self-authenticating; for in such an experience all
things increasingly fit together in a single intelligible whole.

William Temple: *Thoughts on Some problems of the Day*

i

KNUTSFORD JAIL, Hugh was fond of pointing out,
had been condemned as unsuitable by modern standards, so after being used for German prisoners
during the war it was taken over as a Test School for Ordinands! Conditions were spartan and primitive. The only
method of heating one's cell was by warming a brick over a
gas ring. To mitigate the rigours of winter (it was in January
1922 that he became "the baby" of the school, and it was
snowing hard), Hugh saved the dregs of the evening urns of
tea, boiled them up again on his gas ring and pinned up a
notice offering to deliver early morning tea at 2d. a cup. He
signed the notice "Renraw". The authorities saw through
the naïve disguise and the enterprise was squashed. It was
his first attempt to better his impecunious state as a student.

What Knutsford meant in his development is indicated by
a letter to his father the following year:

"I felt it intensely you sending me that £2 when you must

yourself be just longing for more funds. But I *do* thank you most really, old darling Dad. With this money I was able to go up to Swanwick for the Knutsford Fellowship Conference, and the three days there have been extraordinarily helpful to me in getting my vision of my vocation ever so much broader. I came to realize there the narrowness of our outlook on Christianity—the awful narrowness of even the clergy, so many of them today. You see, Knutsford stood for breadth of vision, though it was not till this conference that I have begun to realize the full implications of Christianity in its widest and most universal expression."

The "Chief" of Knutsford at that time was F. R. Barry,[1] whose book, *The Relevance of Christianity,* later emphasized this universal application of our Faith to every department of life. It was a completely new idea to Hugh. So far his religion, derived from his family background and evangelical upbringing, had been a matter of personal piety. It had not occurred to him that it had any bearing on social or other problems. One might say that his Christianity hitherto had been a matter of lineage; but a line, after all, has direction but no breadth. Now it was as if a whole new dimension had opened out. "It always brings me up with a rather sudden bump," he wrote several years later from a student conference at High Leigh, "when I get amongst my non-college friends and relations, and realize how prejudiced the ordinary person is. I was brought up in an atmosphere in which one simply didn't talk about R.C.'s except to refer to their 'idolatry'. I suppose it's in the same class as the attitude of the old 'Verbiles'[2] to the S.C.M. For example, the day we leave here a conference of the Officers' (Army) Christian Union comes in, and already orders have come through that

---

[1] Now Bishop of Southwell.
[2] Hugh's favourite name for "Fundamentalists".

all S.C.M. books in the library are to be removed; indeed, that practically the whole of the bookshop here should be closed down."

The closed shop and the closed mind could never be Hugh's after Knutsford. It was there he first learned to think. "The great thing I owe to the Chief," he frequently said, "was that he taught us to ask the question 'Is it TRUE?' That's the important thing; not is it Catholic? or is it Evangelical? or is it helpful? or even does it work? but 'Is it TRUE?'"

That was the seed sown at Knutsford. Oxford and S.C.M. and William Temple would nourish it, but F. R. Barry implanted it, and to him Hugh was ever grateful. He, in his turn, was fond of his youngest student, and in the Easter vacation generously took Hugh with him for a holiday to Italy, where they visited Rome and the picture galleries of Florence and spent a never-to-be-forgotten Easter in Assisi. Hugh found in Italy a whole new world of beauty, which led him to choose Greek sculpture for his special subject the following year at Oxford.

Though younger than the other Knutsford men, Hugh was further advanced than most of them in his studies, having been pursuing the Classics while they were fighting in the trenches. Consequently, while most of them were "going back to school" under the various tutors, Hugh was doing more advanced work with "the Chief", who was anxious that he should go up to Oxford and read "Greats". He entered him for his own college, Oriel, but the entrance examination had to be taken for another college at the same time, and it was here that Hugh discovered that the Knutsford outlook was not approved in some ecclesiastical circles; for the Dean made it quite clear that he had little use for Knutsford men, and turned him down accordingly.

At Oriel, however, he was successful, and there he took up residence in the Michaelmas Term of 1922, eager to pursue further the question which Knutsford had taught him to ask—"Is it true?" And at the same time his future wife, waiting for the train to take her for her first term to Oxford, was listening to her Father-in-God, Bishop John Owen of St David's, earnestly exhorting her to remember that the prime requisite for "Greats" is Intellectual Honesty.

ii

Intellectual honesty! That was the trouble; for now the growing pains began. Plunged from an evangelical home background and the school for ordinands into the critical, agnostic atmosphere of undergraduate life, meeting for the first time men of every sort of religious belief and of none, it is not surprising that he began to question his own sense of vocation and wonder if it had all been a mistake. His mother had always been critical of the Church of England and thought it out of touch with both God and man. She could not feel at home in its services, and she had a burning sense of social responsibility which to her mind was lacking in the conventional churchgoers of the Cape. Was she right, Hugh wondered. Was the Church out of touch with reality? It hadn't seemed so at Knutsford, but so far in Oxford he had not come across that "universal" outlook on Christianity among the other Christians of his college; and the non-Christians, in their superior way, gave one to understand that no intelligent people believed the Christian doctrines nowadays. What added to his distress was the knowledge that he owed his place at the University to the Church's ordination grant. Wasn't it dishonest to take it? But could he throw it up and go down? Or should he go through with it and then choose another profession and earn enough to pay it all back?

These doubts were not voiced in his letters home, but a rather verbose effusion of his second term partly shows the way his mind was working. ". . . I've had tea several times in X's rooms (he is going to be a parson) discussing things about which we have very different opinions. He has a rather quick temper, but is awfully good-natured, his great failing being *narrow-mindedness;* he just doesn't see the awful misery of the world and can't see why an undergrad should trouble himself about other people's misfortunes. He thinks there is simply *nothing* wrong with the Church as it is today . . . I tried to show him that this is *all wrong,* that the Church must be a great *throbbing, bursting, loving* brotherhood of REAL MEN AND WOMEN who recognize that their fellow men are all temples of the Holy Spirit. . . . Christ did not die that there might be an excuse for some emotionally minded people to form a self-admiration *clique* and forget the WORLD. However, in spite of our differences we are very great friends. . . . Then there's Y, who has served for some years as an Army officer during the war in India and feels that the C. of E. does not cut ice and that there is something vastly more important for it to do than exhort people to come to church as an end in itself. . . . It seems to me that we must begin at the other end and *give a lead* in every normal activity of ordinary people, and so convince people by example of the SANITY of Christianity. You see, Y knows there is a wealth of healthy experience which the Church has not penetrated. I suppose it *is* tending nowadays to face up to social problems—it certainly will have to. But X does not see this point of view. I rather think he says, 'Let other people look to the slums, while I look after the respectible (*sic*) Christians.' I do hope I'm not seeming to be a prig or anything of that sort, but I am telling you this, Mum, in all confidence, and so hope you will understand."

Similarly, when canvassing college opinion on the subject of formal chapel services, he exclaims in exasperation, "How chronically conservative some people are, especially religious ones! No wonder the others say they haven't time to dawdle about with Christianity if that's what it means."

Although his daily office came to mean much to Hugh as a priest, yet throughout his ministry he never lost sight of the outsider's point of view. He knew that to beginners the Prayer Book services need far more explanation than is realized by those born and bred in the Church. In time he learned patience and tolerance even with the "chronically conservative", but in his Oxford days he found his faith in the Church quite as sorely tried by the conventionally religious as by the heretics and agnostics.

It was in the midst of this turmoil of spirit that William Temple, Bishop of Manchester, came to speak to the Student Christian Movement in Oxford on "The Universality of Christ", the theme of the projected C.O.P.E.C.[1] Conference of which he was chairman; and Hugh, listening to him, found his doubts resolved. Through William Temple's eyes he saw the real Church, militant here on earth, going out to bring the love of God into every relationship of men. He always looked back on this as the real turning-point in his life, for Temple's brilliant intellect and straightforward faith had exploded the assumption that no intelligent person could still be a Christian; and his kind of Christianity made sense. Hugh began to read *Mens Creatrix,* while he threw himself into the S.C.M. and preparations for C.O.P.E.C.

[1] Conference on Politics, Economics, and Citizenship—Birmingham 1924.

Writing to his mother again, he fills page after page with the ideas that are seething in his mind about all the subjects of the C.O.P.E.C. syllabus: education, penal reform, the home, property, leisure, the relation of the sexes. "In my opinion a parson should have a thorough understanding of all these and other problems at his finger-tips." A tall order! "People don't realize that Christianity must mean all or nothing. This wide, broad conception of Christianity that overrides all differences of belief in different Christian bodies, and unites us in one tremendous onward move, Christianizing every jolly thing from the individual to the empires of the world in the conviction that the laws of love and fellowship in Christ are the only ones which are going to make the world 'make sense'—this is the Gospel I intend to begin spreading."

The exuberant style of youth might mellow, but he never lost sight of the vision. "Christianizing every jolly thing" might well be called the motto of his ministry.

He goes on to meet his mother's misgivings about the relevance of an academic, classical education: "After this very inadequate sketch" (eight pages or so) "of Christianity as I conceive it—humble and intensely *real continual* communion with God, blossoming forth into reforms which shall 'turn the world upside down', as St Paul did in a world very like our own today, I don't think, Mother, you can feel you want to ask 'what is the practical use of the training I am going through now'. Problems of twentieth century civilization won't be solved by C3 brains! The need, in this generation, is for Leaders, not sheep. And a leader *must* be right abreast with the advance guard of KNOWLEDGE in all its branches and able to compete with the best (non-Christian) intellects. Do you realize that whereas before the war it was thought extremely bad to have less than 700 ordinands in training a year, today the number is 300! . . . If ever there was a crisis, here it is. It is a call to every man who has the mental powers to use them to the full. No, Mum, I *must* WORK!"

Work he certainly did, and how he found time for the mammoth letters home is a puzzle, for his afternoons were spent on the river, where he had been chosen for the college eight, and he was spending much time and energy on his social projects.

As Honour Mods. loomed nearer he began to curtail his activities. "I'm withdrawing from the Oxford and Bermondsey Club and other societies until I have got 'schools' over. I am only going to run a Social and International Problems Study Group in Oriel and have one meeting a week. I'm going to try to keep the groups small so that they may remain *study* groups and not develop into debating societies."

For the time being his own study had to be concentrated on catching up with his Greek and Latin texts, for he could never command much leisure for reading in the vacations. To eke out his University grant, he regularly took tutoring posts to keep himself when not at college. True, he stipulated for four hours to himself each day for reading, but they were hard to come by; when his charges had retired to bed their elders had a way of confiding their problems and difficulties to the young tutor. It was extraordinary how, even at that age, he seemed to attract confidences and inspire confidence. Not for nothing had his nickname at his prep. school been "Grandpa"! "How *wise* he was," wrote a member of one family he stayed with, ". . . and how discreet! And how finely he coped with difficult situations." Good training, doubtless, for a parish priest, but something of a handicap to scholarship.

29

He was busy writing to his young sisters in South Africa, drawing up a scheme of reading for the elder, who was just leaving school, and offering to set her essays on the books he suggested. "We can't be little ignoramusses, you know, in this exciting modern world." The younger one was being confirmed, and he writes to her: "So many people lose patience when you begin discussing 'doctrine'. They much prefer to feel and know what a wonderful experience it is to be a Christian than solemnly sit down and take it to bits and try to put it into unromantic words. And I don't blame them. Unfortunately, however, you've got to have something definite to which you can point and say, 'When it's all boiled down, that's what I believe in, only it's miles more exciting really than it looks on paper.' That's really what Creeds are."

His letters to his parents now had another exciting theme: the imminent arrival of a new baby brother. "How lucky the girls are to be on the spot, for I do *love* little babies, as you know," and the theme inspires a lyrical outburst: "What crowds of thoughts the arrival of a new baby calls up! Love seems just at the root of all that's fine in life; love issues in better houses for slum-folk, love issues in peace between nations, love issues in sincerity in dealing with our fellow men, and love issues in the advent of a new soul to take up the challenge of Christ. What a lot of ways Love has of expressing itself! I don't suppose mine will ever express itself in a family. I think it will consist in showing other people how to love each other. That will need all my undivided energies and freedom to throw myself into the world of 'lust, oppression, crime' and by God's strength rescue some of it from all the shams, unrealities and sordidness. It's an awfully big task, but I'm longing to have a shot, anyway!"

A prophetic glimpse of Marriage Guidance and Moral Welfare. Showing people how to love each other: could there be a better description of that work which he made specially his own? It is, perhaps, natural that in those early days he should have seen the task as demanding the freedom of celibacy. Looking forward, he would have been startled to see a national daily newspaper summing up his life-work under the headline "Marriage was his success". Looking back, it is plain that the distinctive contribution he was to make could only have been made by a family man.

John was born on New Year's Day, "Mods" was safely over in March, and Hugh's letters in the summer term of 1924 are full of the joy of coming to grips at last with "Greats" work, and of an incredible number of S.C.M. and other activities, especially the organizing of parties of students to be conducted round the worst slums of his parish by the rector of St Aldate's, "Chavasse[1]—an admirable fellow!" "But through all these activities I am trying *hard* to find a way of coming out to you in July. ... . In desperation, I went out and sold 15s. of my Mods books with which I have finished and used the money to insert an advertisement in the personal column of *The Times:* 'Oxford undergraduate desires charge of child or invalid to (and from) S. Africa, July. Thoroughly capable and experienced.' 15s. only means 3 lines!"

Alas! the advertisement did not prove more successful than his many other inquiries, and the lady with a child of three who answered it was extremely indignant at finding the advertiser was of the male sex. She could not know that even at the age of six he was quite equal to "looking after the little girls". "It's awfully disappointing. You can't think how much I've been longing to see you all. We would have

[1] Now Bishop of Rochester.

31

had such fun together. Well, well, we must just make the best of it and things will work out all right."

Unexpectedly Dr Phelps, the Provost, sent for him. "What's all this about you trying to work your passage to South Africa?" Hugh explained that he had not seen his family for over two years and that he was very anxious to spend his twenty-first birthday with them and to make the acquaintance of his new brother. "How much is the passage?" asked the Provost. Hugh told him. "It's a refreshing change in these days," observed Dr Phelps, "to find a young man who will really take such trouble to go home and see his family"; and he wrote out a cheque for the full amount. "I just don't understand the things that happen to me," Hugh said wonderingly. Perhaps the Provost's letter to his father after the trip was over provides some explanation:

ORIEL COLLEGE,

OXFORD.

26 *Oct.* 24.

DEAR MR WARNER,

Your son is back safe and sound, looking all the better for his time with you and very happy in the retrospect of it. You ask me what I think of him. Well, he is pure gold. I would trust him anywhere. He is very patriotic to his college; a thoroughly good influence and enjoys the respect and affection of us all.

Very truly yrs,

L. R. PHELPS

This summer vacation in his native Africa confirmed in Hugh two things: his love of babies and his hatred of slums. His mother was in the thick of her epic fight for the District Nurse and took him with her to visit some of the worst cases of native misery. He never forgot the trek out to the veldt to

32

take some soup to a poor mother who, for lack of any human accommodation, had taken refuge in an abbatoir.

But he was concerned, too, for his mother herself, who was in a sad state of nervous exhaustion, quite unable to stand the incessant crying of her seven-months-old baby suffering from teething troubles, weaning, and her own overwrought state. Hugh had a magic touch with babies, and many a night of that African summer did he take his small frantic brother and calm him to sleep in his arms. The time would come when the rôles would be reversed, and John's hand would soothe the irritation of his last illness.

It was on this visit home, also, that Hugh first came in touch with another life-long interest of his—Divine Healing. Mr Hickson had recently held his famous healing mission in George, and friends and acquaintances had impressive stories to tell him. Mrs Warner, with her usual impetuosity, had been caught up on a wave of enthusiasm and wanted Hugh to give first place to this in his S.C.M. work. But he was not to be side-tracked like that. On his return to Oxford he contributed an article on the subject to the S.C.M. magazine, *The Student Movement,* but a letter to his mother puts it in its context as just a part of the Christian faith which it is his vocation to preach. The Church must teach the power of prayer, he emphasizes, to change the *whole* of life, social as well as personal, moral as well as physical. We must not encourage people to cramp their religion by concentrating their prayers on physical health and "thinking what wonderful people we are". For him "preaching Christ" would mean something much wider in which Divine Healing would be one important element.

Honour Mods. being over, and "Greats" comfortably far ahead, Hugh's third year at Oxford was becoming crowded with activities. He was Captain of Boats for Oriel, and Social Study Secretary for the S.C.M., and in November 1934 he attended a meeting in London of study secretaries from many other universities and colleges, at which he was asked to explain the scheme of study and practical work he had evolved for use in Oxford. "They all seemed to think it was helpful," he told his mother, "and asked if they might take a copy of it back to their own Universities and try to run a scheme on the same lines." A paragraph appended to his programme for a week-end conference is worthy of note: "Each group will be asked to be prepared to read a paper (15 minutes) to the Conference on some specified aspect of their own particular problem. *Facts* should fill the greater part of the papers." Theories, opinion, and "hot air" were at a discount in Hugh's study circles. "Is it true?" was the criterion of his research.

But his religion was not all a matter of "works". "Seven of us in Oriel have begun a prayer circle among ourselves once a week . . . quite informal. I feel quiet personal prayer must be right at the root of our everyday lives, and it's so easy for it to get crowded out. There is so much hurry and scurry trying to do 'practical Christianity' in our social work and study, our meetings and conferences. These (prayer) meetings are a great help in making us see these activities in their right perspective."

Mr Chavasse, of St Aldate's, wrote to the Rector of Broxbourne, "Warner is considered one of the leading lights in the S.C.M. and I see a great future before him. Also I believe his convictions are becoming more distinctly evangelical as he tests things here in Oxford." This must not be taken to indicate that Hugh was becoming a party man—a thing which he detested. "If only we could get away from cliques, churchiness and party spirit!" he wrote to his mother. "In the S.C.M. we are trying to bring people of different views together and make them *think*."

At St Aldate's he met many missionary-minded, outward-looking Christians such as Alec Fraser's family and the Achimota set, and there he recovered his own sense of vocation.

"I can't help wondering sometimes whether I am worth all these blessings that seem to have been tumbling about me for the last six years," he wrote to his father, ". . . and what in the end I will be called upon to do. One thing I do know, and feel very real, and that is whatever I am called to do will be as an ordained man." There were no further doubts about that.

His philosophical studies were going forward under his tutor, W. D., afterwards Sir David, Ross, the great moral philosopher, from whom he learned the fundamental distinction between act and motive, between Right and Good— in short, between sin and sinner—so essential for his later moral welfare work. When, in November 1933 Ross's translation of Aristotle's *Nicomachean Ethics* was published, he obtained an autographed copy, which he presented as a birthday gift to a fellow "Greats" student at Lady Margaret Hall, who was President of the Women's S.C.M. Only Hugh, surely, would choose a treatise on ethics for his first courting present.

iii

"Paradise was not complete until there was Eve to bring love into it." This remark is ascribed, astonishingly, to Miss Wordsworth, first Principal of Lady Margaret Hall. It must have startled the male dons to whom it was addressed, doubtful as they were of the wisdom of admitting a women's college into their Oxford paradise. This chapter of Hugh's life would not be complete either if it chronicled merely the philosophy and rowing and left out the poetry and romance. The point is of some importance in recording the influences which went to make Hugh Warner the man he was, and determined his characteristic approach to the business of "showing people how to love each other".

"Love, in the sense of romantic literature," wrote his old Chief, F. R. Barry, in *The Relevance of Christianity,* "is a rapturous moment of exaltation succeeded by either remorse or boredom. Love as Christianity understands it is a thing that grows, through mutual companionship, shared interests and common sacrifices, into a union of personalities." Hugh would endorse and even underline that, but he would somehow, in his inimitable way, make it sound more exciting. It is this life-long "growing together", he would emphasize later in his talks to youth clubs or engaged couples, which is the genuine romance; and to no lesser ideal would he yield the monopoly of rapture and exaltation!

As for the growth, Hugh loved to sum up its early stages as "We met at our first Swanwick,[1] fell in love at our second, and got engaged at our third!"—an over-simplification which nevertheless indicates that the start was uncertain and the progress slow. Those of Hugh's friends who were beginning to remark that "there must be some attraction at Lady Margaret Hall" were puzzled at first to know which or who the attraction was, and none was more baffled and uncertain than the attraction herself. The puzzle was due to Hugh's own characteristic approach to women. He had always an unselfconscious and friendly ease of manner, combined with a naturally courteous attitude towards all the

[1] The annual summer conference of the S.C.M. at Swanwick in Derbyshire.

opposite sex. Moreover, as President of the S.C.M. he was known to be concerned for closer and friendlier co-operation between the men's and women's committees. This bee in his bonnet, as it was considered by his fellows on the men's committee, was a source of some entertainment to them, and they could not resist pulling his leg a little, as appears in a letter written by a still uncertain young woman to a confidante after that second Swanwick.

"On Monday we went for an expedition to Wingfield Manor—the whole (or nearly the whole) Oxford contingent, 47 in all, about equally divided as to sexes. It was pouring with rain, but Hugh assured us that 'it was only half an hour's walk at his pace, and an hour's at Mrs. Fraser's!' and that we should have tea and cream in a nice dry crypt when we got there, and that we *must* all come because he had ordered tea for 50 and would be about £5 down if we didn't turn up!

"The four of us led off at a terrific pace. (Very correct! The two present and two past presidents.) By the way, there are plenty of suitable subjects here for him to practise his 'friendly relations between the sexes' on, and I'm under no illusions. . . . We steamed along, and after about an hour's walking through banks and braes, bogs and ditches, we arrived panting at 'The erstwhile picturesque residence where the beautiful Queen of Scots beat her wings like a caged bird against the relentless walls", as Hugh's guidebook so poetically expressed it. When we had all collected we sat down amidst the wet and muddy ruins, while Hugh gave us 'excerpts' from the guidebook and some historical instruction. Then he marched us all to the top of a tower, with a stiff spiral staircase. I counted the steps, there were 88! . . . After that we were taken up another tower and down again, and then to tea in the crypt, where there was a long trestle table round which we sat alternately, man, woman, etc.

"After tea we all sat round in a circle and enjoyed an impromptu entertainment, provided chiefly by John Maud—the son of the Bishop of Kensington—a priceless comic turn! After various absurd songs accompanied by a ukelele, he added some impromptu verses of his own about Conference personalities, the last one being

Twenty Oxford women, twenty Oxford boys,
The men do the thinking the women make the noise.
Why we've all been brought together here is not quite clear,
But some of Mr Warner's tent have a Very Bright Idea!

"Whereupon G. S. jumped up and recited:

A terrible flirter called Hugh
Said this is the thing we must do,
We must walk male and female
All up hill and down dale,
Till the Kingdom of Heaven comes true!

"Poor Hugh! But he just said cheerfully, 'Thank you! Next please . . .'

"P.S.—I suppose you know Hugh has just been elected Chairman of the General Committee. When he came into the room to take the chair at the first meeting, Zoë Fairfield remarked, *sotto voce,* 'The standard of looks in the S.C.M. is going up!'"

No one could fail to remark Hugh Warner's physical appearance in the full glow, as he was then, of youth and beauty. And lest "beauty" should seem a biassed or exaggerated estimate, there is on record a surprising exchange of notes at an Educational Committee meeting, between the Principal of Lady Margaret Hall and the Headmistress of

Roedean, who had not known that the young woman she had recently offered a place on her staff was likely to forsake the teaching profession for matrimony. "Are you very angry about Nancy Owen's engagement?" "Not at all. Who is the young man?" "Hugh Warner, of Oriel." "What is he like?" "Almost *too* beautiful for a man!"

In the March of 1926 two young people who saw their final examinations looming ahead, and felt that studies had suffered somewhat seriously of late, each determined independently to put all distracting thoughts out of their heads and stay up in Oxford through the Easter vac. to do some serious work. And each discovered that the other had done the same! "There's a divinity that shapes our ends. . . ." The happy ending, or rather happy beginning, came on 21 March, "the first day of Spring", as Hugh never failed to recall in yearly letters and presents on his betrothal date, which he always kept as devotedly as his wedding anniversary. But he was right, too, when he stated that he got engaged at his third "Swanwick", for it was not until then that the engagement was made public. "Greats" must come first (so notes and meetings were severely rationed), and he was anxious, too, to wait until his family were home. His mother's health had once more necessitated her return from Africa, and his father, though not due to retire for another year or two, had decided to send the rest of the family on ahead.

It was obvious that marriage would have to wait for a long time, as also would ordination; the immediate necessity was to pay back the debt owing to his college, for in spite of tutoring jobs his years at the University had been a drain on his resources, especially as he had been steadily sending home gifts of odd pounds from time to time "to help pay the doctor's bill", "to keep the girls at school a bit longer", "to give Mother a birthday free from worry", and the like. He had been offered the post of Inter-collegiate Secretary for the S.C.M. in Birmingham University for the next three years (he subsequently asked that the appointment be reduced to two years), and with that, and continuing his tutoring in the vacations, and his fiancée's teaching salary, there would be some hope of saving for a home.

All these self-denying ordinances will ring strangely in the ears of present-day couples, to whom six months is a "long" engagement. But the prospect of a long wait cast no cloud over that last term at Oxford, nor, when it came to the point, did "Greats"; for Hugh, as would always be his way when changes impended, had his eyes on the next objective, and passed the one he had been aiming for so long almost without noticing it. An elderly tutor, contemplating the lists in which both had achieved a Second, spoke the final, if unexpected, word on Hugh's academic career: "It's the most satisfactory thing I've seen. I'd rather see you two together in any class than either one in the First without the other!"

In the work Hugh Warner was to do, a happy marriage was as vital an ingredient as a degree in moral philosophy. Oxford had given him both.

3

WIDENING CIRCLES

Birmingham, S.C.M.

The Eastern Orthodox Church has the box with the healing gifts needed by the disunited Christians. But the key is in the hands of the West, and the time has come when it must be opened.

Nicolas Zernov: *The Reintegration of the Church*

i

IT is difficult to draw the line between the chapters of Hugh Warner's life, for before one was really finished he was already half-way into the next. There was always the narrowest of margins between his engagements, so that the General Strike of 1926, which caused all the examinations of the summer term to be postponed a fortnight, upset his closely planned diary, and mid-June, which should have seen him taking up his new work as S.C.M. Secretary, found him still at Oxford taking his final "Schools". He wasted no time, however, the minute his last paper was finished in speeding straight from Oxford to a series of conferences and committees, returning for a flying visit for his *viva voce*, en route for the annual Swanwick conference, at which this year he was to be Chairman. Nothing could show more vividly the speed with which the new chapter had caught up on the old, than the modest little "viva" fitted in, almost by the way, to his diary's jig-saw puzzle of dates.

At Swanwick Hugh stepped easily into the rôle of leadership and showed his qualities as a chairman, as his friend,

Tom Craske, now Bishop of Gibraltar, has recalled: "I remember vividly his tall, slim, attractive, upright figure, clad in immaculate white cricket shirt and blue shorts; his genial but firm control of that large gathering of 600 students, and his conduct of the conference prayers, which were always clear and appropriate."

There followed conferences at Karlovsci in Yugo-Slavia and at Nyborg in Denmark, at which were hammered out the status and future of the I.S.S.[1] and its relationship to the World's Student Christian Federation. As Chairman of the S.C.M. General Committee, Hugh was one of the British delegates; "up to my eyes in work, speaking, pouring oil (most of all), writing minutes of everything." But it would not have been Hugh if he had not found time to send vivid descriptions and impressions to his father in Africa, his mother and "the Bank" folk, and also now to his fiancée. From Karlovsci he sent a photograph. It is typical that it should show him sitting in the middle of a bunch of children, with a small girl holding on to each arm.

"It's extraordinary how much a smile can do," he says in a letter. "Thank heavens *it* hasn't to be translated! Imagine your three or four interpreters solemnly rising up in turn to reproduce it in French, German, etc.!"

Letters were written in the train and in all sorts of odd moments, and a steady stream of postcards marked the stopping-places along the route for Nyborg. A picture of Feuerbach's "Orpheus and Eurydice" bears a long message headed "Written while standing in the street. Vienna, 4th Aug." and ends, "*Must move on.*" "You should frame that!" remarked his fiancée's family wickedly. "It's so typical of Hugh . . . the earnest 'upward and onward' ex-

---

[1] International Student Service, which in 1925 had superseded the European Student Relief of post-war years.

pression of Orpheus; and you could write underneath, "Must move on!"

It was the true word spoken in jest; for it was now that the "upward" direction was added to the "onward" in Hugh's development. The narrow line of boyish personal devotion had been broadened out into a "world-wide" view of the Church. But if his Christianity was not to remain earthbound, swamped in schemes for social improvement, he needed the third dimension of "height", the glimpse of the Heavenlies, of the worship of a Church rooted in Eternity, which burst upon him fully for the first time this summer through his contact, in a Russian settlement in Belgrade, with the *émigrés* of the Orthodox Church. The experience balanced the check given to his optimism by the tragic conditions in the Balkans, where realizing the ideals of C.O.P.E.C. would clearly be no easy matter. One might put it another way and say that whereas his early training had equated religion with moral goodness, and Knutsford had taught him the absolute value of truth, Orthodox worship made explicit what, even as a child, he had sensed implicitly, that beauty is essentially part of the Vision of God. "I'm *so* glad you are in touch with Sonia Zernov, and with Orthodox thinking," he wrote a year later to his fiancée, who had met one of the same Russian *émigrés* in France. "It has been very inspiring to me—their sanely but beautifully mystical approach to things of the spirit. . . . I feel the Orthodox Churches have something of tremendous value to give us 'Protestants'; their emphasis on the liturgy, their *standing* for hours and hours on end, as the position for worship in the presence of God; their grasp of the Whole, instead of parts (so typical of Protestantism proper). *Do* get her to talk to you about what she means by the Church. The little that I have learnt from Orthodoxy has meant an awful lot to me—more than any other single experience through the Church. Isn't it that we Protestants are too self-conscious, thinking more of respectability than of childlike surrender to God? Perhaps because all their earthly props and standbys have failed, the vision of God of these *émigrés* seems to belong to another world of expression, transcending all our arguments—but *so* difficult to explain to people who do not appreciate the *poetry* of religion. . . . Maybe a critical faculty is *not* one of their strong points. . . . What miles we've got to go before Reunion, and what do we expect Reunion is going to mean, anyway? Even the C. of E. does not suggest, as yet, the real answer. Sometimes I think the French are true in their description of us English, 'faisants leur nid dans une contradiction.' And yet—why not a nest in the fork of a tree?"

Hugh's own critical faculty was getting him into some trouble at the Conference at Nyborg Strand, where he was asked to open the first of three plenary sessions on "Evangelism". "I said that with the majority of students in G.B. today the word itself conjured up all that was most objectionable to them in religion—short cuts *via* emotion, and so on. Such words as 'salvation', 'saved by the Blood of the Lamb', 'conversion', and most of the conventional phrases meant nothing to them. A student's thought today is essentially synthetic, and he wants to see life as an intellectual whole, built up after the pattern he has followed in his science and philosophy, but in practice he is left with his 'school religion'—an immature babe, while all other sides of his life are growing and developing in all directions; so it seems irrelevant and he dismisses it from his mind. . . . I had not realized how foreign such ideas are to the Continentals. Germany got up and lamented my 'psychological' emphasis; Russia asked 'Which Christ was I preaching?';

Robert Wilder booked me for a long talk on my spiritual life . . . and so on. On the other hand, America, Canada, New Zealand, Australia, S. Africa, and India and China at different times said '*Thank you*'!"

As a consequence Hugh found himself, somewhat against his will, elected chairman of a group into which the younger and critical element of the conference had formed themselves, and pushed forward for election on to the Executive Committee in competition with the oldest and most experienced members there; an awkward situation which again called into play his capacity for "pouring oil". But the net result was that he was unhesitatingly chosen as one of the W.S.C.F. delegates to visit the U.S.A. the following May.

ii

Hugh's predecessor as S.C.M. President in Oxford, Gerald Streatfield, had done some tutoring for the Shuttleworth family, to whom he was distantly related, and being asked to find a successor, had passed the job on to Hugh, thereby relieving him for some four years of the recurrent search for holiday employment. Lord Shuttleworth's son and heir had been killed in action in 1917, and the grandsons spent most of their school holidays with their grandfather and their "Aunt Rachel" at Barbon Manor, which one of them would have inherited had not the next war claimed them both as victims. Besides these two boys, a host of other grandchildren, cousins, aunts and nannies collected from time to time at Barbon, and Hugh would find himself in charge of a schoolroom full of assorted ages. One Christmas there were eleven to be instructed and entertained ("I feel like the Pied Piper," he wrote); and one summer he took four of the boys camping on the fells, revelling, as always, in the becks, the waterfalls and the skies of Westmorland, after the terms spent in industrial Birmingham.

For Lord Shuttleworth, who had been a member of Gladstone's Cabinet, he had a high regard and respect, and the old man's reminiscences opened a new window for him on the world of politics, education and literary society. (There was the exciting evening when, going through old letters, they came upon one in the handwriting and with the signature of Charlotte Brontë.) "Aunt Rachel" (she became that to Hugh immediately) later embroidered an exquisite set of stoles for his ordination, and an amusing letter consults him about the emblems to be used. ". . . Do you know what the emblem of St Hugh of Lincoln is? Or is there any other St Hugh, *par exemple* St Hugh of Grenoble, whom you would prefer to regard as your Patron Saint? Both of these seem to have been Bishops and Carthusians, and one built Lincoln Cathedral and the other the Grande Chartreuse. I see that St Hugh of Grenoble, by the sign of the Cross, when short of fasting food, changed some fowls into tortoises, and so got over the difficulty. Is his emblem a tortoise? This would hardly be suitable." Hardly, perhaps, for a stole; but for Hugh, calm, deliberate, with a disconcerting way of forging directly ahead and beating the quicker-witted to the post, it would not be inappropriate.

iii

Canon Tatlow, in *The History of the Student Christian Movement,* has described the function of an Inter-collegiate Secretary as rather that of a pastor or chaplain. "None of us realized," so he writes, "when the secretaryships were first instituted, the amount of individual and intimate help and guidance those who held them would give. . . ."

At first the new Inter-collegiate Secretary for Birmingham was a little uncertain of his rôle and feeling his way somewhat tentatively in his new surroundings. Living in "digs" and having no real footing in the University, he hardly knew where to begin. The first thing seemed to be to attach himself to some faculty and become a genuine student himself, and to begin with he thought of studying medicine. This was not a new idea. As a boy he had been attracted to it and had found it hard to choose between the relative merits of a doctor's and a parson's calling: he often wished he could combine the two. He was particularly anxious to get into the medical faculty, as so few of them belonged to the S.C.M. "Medical students seem to be either 'verbiles' or agnostics," he noted.

The registrar pointed out that the course would be too long for him and would take up too much of his time, *and* money. "In the end I've decided to do Experimental Psychology. Having delved into the philosophic side of psychology, it will be awfully interesting and useful to see it on the practical and educative side."

It was an inspired choice, of enormous value to him later in his work as parish priest, confessor and marriage counsellor. He attended Professor Valentine's lectures, being greatly amused by his detached and objective studies of his own children; indeed, he took a leaf out of the professor's book in this respect when, many years later, he tried out his experiments in film strips and pamphlets on his own family. Fresh from "Greats", he pronounced it "high time psychoanalysts were given a thorough course of *logic* before daring to make their attractive generalizations"! Nevertheless, he welcomed whole-heartedly the light that his studies threw on the often puzzling behaviour of human beings, a subject which always interested him, combining as he did in a

47

remarkable degree a very human sympathy and imagination with an objective and analytical habit of mind. "What a delightfully balanced sort of person he is!" he writes of a certain lecturer. "The result, I'm sure, of having come to a stage of 'understanding' where a knowledge of one's bodily and mental make-up sets one free from inhibitions. So many possibilities open up as soon as one begins to understand how more than wonderfully one is put together—how essentially an 'organism' one is in spite of one's apparently unconnected peculiarities and 'sides'. The more I look around at people I know, the more I see the root cause of their troubles is refusal to face knowing themselves. People are so afraid of the daylight—continually hiding their hopes and fears and pretending what is isn't, and what isn't is. *What* a difference when we look at a thing openly and directly, and see the lip corners turning slowly upwards!" . . .

He had spent his "Greats" prize money on a formidable set of volumes—"Beautiful tomes, happily all the same size, stamped with a beautiful gold Oriel coat of arms, and now looking out at me from a shelf on my revolving bookcase. McDougall is sitting next to Viscount Haldane, mutually discussing *Abnormal Psychology* and the *Pathway to Reality;* cheek to cheek are Burtt and Broad, and what between them they don't know of *The Metaphysical Foundations of Modern Science* and *The Place of the Mind in Nature,* I don't think either of us need trouble our heads about." . . . These, with Whitehead, Temple, and others had to be dissected, discussed and digested in voluminous letters, for Hugh could always do his thinking best on paper and was revelling in having found a correspondent who not only would read his dissertations (his young sisters confess that they skipped them!), but enjoyed replying at length.

48

"Your love-letters," exclaimed his future sister-in-law, "must be as bad as the Brownings'!"

Birmingham was a very different theatre of war from Oxford for an S.C.M. campaign, as Hugh discovered to his dismay at his first Freshers' Social. "Before the dancing, which was the chief part of the function, the President of the Guild announced to the assembled company that they were to hear about the chief University societies from the secretaries of them, each speaker to be allowed three minutes. The Societies were the Athletic, the Dramatic, the Musical, the S.C.M. and the O.T.C.! It certainly made me sit up! But to explain the S.C.M. in three minutes to a cosmopolitan crowd of irresponsible and excited men and women is a task I don't commend to anybody. And I had been given *very* short notice."

No wonder that later in the term, returning from a secretaries' day in London, he wrote: "It was a great inspiration and I have come back with all sorts of good resolutions, but Birmingham has a fatal climatic or atmospheric effect upon such species of resolutions! I have the sense of things slipping through my fingers all the time up here."

The men were scattered in "digs" and occupied in such subjects as mining, engineering and commerce, studies which did not engender criticism, discussion, and the independent reading round the subject he had known at Oxford, but seemed rather to entail an endless copying and writing up of notes. It was difficult to get men of this type into S.C.M. study groups; and a leading business man whom Hugh approached for a subscription warned him against being "visionary" and emphasized the futility of study which is in the air and out of relation to facts. "This is a piece of advice that you can depend will come in some form or another from every business man you interview: rather significant?" It was curious to think that as Social Study Secretary in Oxford he had urged his groups to eschew hot air and stick to facts. Now, in this different mental climate, he was finding the reverse difficulty—to persuade men who were obsessed with facts to do a bit of thinking.

His work during the first two terms brought him interviews with many of the city's leading men, both in business and university life, in connection with an appeal for I.S.S. which had been launched by *The Times,* the Archbishops and the Prime Minister (Stanley Baldwin).

He was conscious, however, that his real work should not be raising money but helping students, and that it was bafflingly difficult to come to grips with it. Boldly he took three important steps. During his second term he left his "digs" and moved, with the generous connivance of the Warden (an Oxford man), into Chancellor's Hall at Edgbaston, the only men's hostel in the University. In spite of the unexpected mid-term intrusion, he was given a friendly welcome, and before long there were few evenings on which some inhabitant of the Hall was not seeking out his room to pour out confidences and problems about emotional tangles, family anxieties or future careers.

A few terms later he was writing: "I was wrong to suggest that Birmingham was 'ducksbackish'. It's because I was thinking in terms of *groups* of people—crowds. One is inclined to think it's more worthwhile to bring off a 'big' meeting than to help *one* fellow with some tangle he may be in; two or three cases in Hall have helped me to see things straighter. . . .

"It has always been the intimate, personal friendships among one's parishioners, when they share their problems with one and feel they can trust one, which has made me look forward to parish work. But somehow I never expected to find this work in the job I'm trying to do here for S.C.M. My S.C.M. experience in Oxford (and it was all I had to build on) seems now very partial and one-sided. Now I'm starting from the other end. The difficulty is to make both ends meet. What most ordinary men and women need is help with their personal lives and to be brought to understand and know Jesus and the Gospel. How far can we expect more or less everybody to be interested in more or less everything—international and racial relations, for instance? . . . One can become a bit of a spiritual dilettante, I'm afraid."

He had tackled racial relations in Oxford by organizing an S.C.M. boycott of a café with a colour bar. Now he realized even more clearly that "international relations" was simply an abstract term for a very personal problem, and he set himself to discover and befriend as many as he could of the 120 foreign students in Birmingham—Egyptians, Persian, Indian, Siamese—many of whom made new and surprising friendships through tea-parties in the Inter-collegiate Secretary's room. The strangest of these visitors was a Japanese Buddhist priest, who had come to England to study Christianity—". . . a delightful old fellow with a strong sense of humour." When Hugh was invited to speak to the St Martin's Mothers' Union on the problem of overseas students in the University, he took "the problem" along with him, in the shape of six or seven foreign students, one of whom, an Indian, he asked to speak for himself about his personal difficulties on coming to England for the first time. The result was many offers of hospitality; ". . . and of course it will mean an awful lot of work getting the plan going really well; but it's all in the game, and immensely worth while."

The second step was equally characteristic, in fact it is a

recurrent motif in his story. It was essential, he felt, in a non-residential University, to have some focal meeting-place and headquarters, and he set to work to acquire for the S.C.M. two derelict rooms over a centrally situated book-shop. By the following year there were study groups meeting in the rooms most evenings of the week, among them a group from the different theological and missionary colleges of various denominations at Selly Oak, Handsworth and Overdale. "Each college is very insular and isolated; a fatal thing for a theological college. I've been working for such a meeting for a long time, and they have agreed to try the experiment of a combined study group for a year."

Before he left Birmingham these clubrooms had become such a success that he was already looking for bigger and better ones. No one was ever surprised when Hugh's "character" was read out of an American self-quiz book popular in his family circle: "You will never reach your goal, and this for a particular reason. Long before you have passed it your eyes have shifted to a further one!"

The third important move was to plan an Easter holiday conference on "Swanwick" lines at Arley Castle in the neighbourhood, an experiment which was repeated the following year. On the second occasion Hugh was persuaded to take the place of a lecturer he had hoped but failed to procure, and himself give the series of addresses planned on Doctrine. It was a change for him to be dealing with theology while someone else led the parallel course on sociology, and he was rather diffident about it. In preparation for it he tried the experiment of taking a small group, six men and six women from among the leaders and possible future leaders of the S.C.M. in the University, away to a quiet Quaker guest-house for a week-end reading party— a new experience for them. The educative value of the small group, with its potentialities of silence and of friendship, in exploring the deeper levels of faith and prayer, was something he was to prove on many a future occasion. "But, look here, I *must* stop. I've got two committee meetings to get along to, a conference to organize, £100 to raise, and five letters to answer." So ends a letter to a relative. Such oases as the quiet week-end were rare.

It was becoming less and less true to say of him in these days that he was "distinctly evangelical"; and he was deeply distressed at the "Protestant" behaviour over the Prayer Book controversy. "To me the thing that hurts most in all this business is the way everything has turned on the subconscious wish for 'exclusion' rather than organic wholeness. I suppose it's always easier to enlist sympathy and enthusiasm *against* things or people rather than a single-minded search for what is true. . . . At least this clarifies the real issue; we have been feeling the increased strain within the Church of England of Catholic and Protestant for the last few years, and this will bring this to a head and force us to examine what we *mean* by Comprehension. . . . I can't bring myself to consider seriously to which group in the Church I belong. I treasure too much the close friendships I find I am continually making by moving among all sorts of different schools of thought, which I know would be impossible if I went about labelled. I keep finding how very close I am to all these different people really, . . . and I always seem to be trying to fit ideas together in a larger context."

iv

An important factor in this development was Hugh's visit to the U.S.A. in May 1927, for the meeting at Lake Mohonk of the Executive Committee of the World's Student Christian Federation. Hugh and Henri Louis Henriod, the Federation General Secretary, were the guests for a few nights in New York of the American Y.M.C.A., and it was arranged that after "Mohonk" they should visit some of the student summer conferences. From the first of these, at Northfield, Mass., Hugh wrote, "I was invited to speak at their 'interest' group on 'The Philosophy of Education' with special reference to Oxford. Oxford is looked up to with awe and deepest reverence by everyone over here as the ideal of all true education (Cambridge, for them, is quite in another category), and it was almost touching the way men have come round me since I talked, to ask me more about Oxford." Another "interest" group was studying "The Church at Home", and he was asked to speak on "The Church as an Inspirational Agency". "I asked each of them what they would consider the really 'inspirational' element in their own church, and with only one exception (an R.C.) they answered 'Preaching', followed by 'Hymns and music' and 'Social gatherings'. Holy Communion was to most of them something extra, valuable but occasional. Prayer, they felt, was rather an introductory 'exercise' to the main business of a service—preaching. The crux of the whole business, I couldn't help feeling, was that the idea of worship—God becoming the centre of all that one is for a brief space—was quite foreign and strange to almost all of them. The rich, pure mysticism of the infant Russian Orthodox Church in emigration stood out all the time against the pragmatic Protestantism over here, in my mind. What a world of difference it would make if we could really bring these big confessions closer together, so that they might overflow into each other and leave the sediment and grounds behind."

From Northfield he went on to a Y.W.C.A. rally of 500 women at Silver Bay on Lake George, where the same subjects seem to have been prominent. "On Friday I had to speak consecutively for 2½ hours—first to a group of 150 on 'English Education', and then straight on to another group of 70 (the one I've been having all the week) on 'The Meaning of Worship'. At the end I felt dead beat. Nothing can be more tiring, I think, than trying to express the inexpressible for well over an hour. But it's curious how closely they followed and how still they kept, in spite of the most uncomfortable positions on the floor, hard chairs and window-sills. We ran right till supper, and 15 minutes after supper I was due to speak to the whole conference in company with Henriod, Mlle. Diétrich, and a Chinese, on the W.S.C.F. I was the last speaker and emphasized the way the W.S.C.F. brings one into touch with the naked facts of tragedy, pain and struggle, physical and spiritual. Americans are so good at making beautiful theories about life from the luxury of an armchair, I think—isolated from the world. It is interesting to see how some of them are beginning to realize this."

"It was 10.30 when my little turn was over, and as I came from the meeting someone came up and asked me to excuse the shortness of notice, but would I take Conference Prayers tomorrow (*i.e.* today) morning at 8.45 a.m. I was feeling rather fagged out with it all, but I went away alone to the side of the lake and felt ever so much refreshed. It was a very still night, the lapping of small waves at my toes was the only sound, and like a dark mass the opposite hills seemed to be very close and over-towering; little pinpricks of light came and went with the movement of the wavelets —phosphorescent small animals, I expect. For a long time it was quite still, then the branches over my head began to move and the wavelets to get more excited, and sweeping along over the lake came the wind—'our Brother the Wind' —gathering force every minute. . . . When at last I went to bed and left the lake all still again as I had found it, you were opening your eyes to the morning and a new day, and I hope that day has been specially happy and beautiful. Anyhow, this morning when I took the service I didn't feel afraid at all, but made it a service of Worship and Silence." Those who saw Hugh's life as one mad rush only saw one-half of the picture.

To the envy of their fellow-delegates and of the students at Northfield and Silver Bay, none of whom had done the 2,000-mile journey across the plains to the "Rockies", Hugh and Henriod were now bound for Colorado, to a Senior Y.M.C.A. Conference at Estes Park, at which a seven-year struggle of the students' department to become autonomous and more like the British S.C.M. was to end successfully. It was an important moment in the history of that movement. It was an equally important moment in the development of Hugh Warner; for it was at Denver, Colorado, that he met Judge Ben Lindsay, whose book, *The Revolt of Youth*, had created a sensation on both sides of the Atlantic with its advocacy of "companionate marriage". After an interview with him Hugh wrote : "A big fact in life over here is the breakdown of marriage which, anyhow at first sight, cuts right across hitherto accepted views. In some respects it has good points in it, including a fuller realization of what Love means, but the extremists are going to very great lengths, which I can't help feeling are ultimately self-contradictory. It's a huge question, and one which people have got to face up to, over *here* at least, very candidly and sincerely." Before he had reached middle age we were having to face up to it over here also; that he was able to take a lead in doing so was partly due to the fact that he had got a start of the problem in Denver in 1927. Only a year later he was writing from Birmingham, of the student situation, "We have to realize that traditions are in the melting-pot everywhere, and that a new pattern of behaviour has to be worked out before new traditions come to be."

V

The British S.C.M. had also reached a turning-point in its history with the impending retirement from the leadership of Canon Tatlow and Miss Fairfield, and Hugh was a member of a remarkable Re-organization Committee, which, like most committees of which he was ever a live member, went far beyond its terms of reference.[1] "It's curious," he wrote, "to compare what I feel about the Student Movement 'crisis' with what one feels about the Prayer Book crisis and the world situation in general. Everywhere new wine seems to be bursting the old bottles. We must be sure of the way we believe things are meant to develop, and the contribution we bring to the Church must essentially have in it the elements of universality so conspicuously absent in some sections of it. Every time I go away from England, even for a short time, I get a bigger vision of my ideal Church of England—the bridge Church, the focus of unity of Protestant, Catholic and Orthodox."

"Even for a short time" refers to two visits to Paris, one to a meeting to deal with a crisis in the French S.C.M., and one to the Committee of Intellectual Co-operation of the League of Nations. Each time Francis Miller (the Chairman of W.S.C.F.) had wired from the Geneva office to have Warner released from his home job for the occasion.

Meanwhile in Birmingham his home job was bearing fruit, in new clubrooms for the University S.C.M. and in a

[1] *The Story of the Student Christian Movement*, by Tissington Tatlow, p. 828.

new atmosphere in Chancellor's Hall, where a new Warden, hitherto antipathetic to religion, sent for Hugh and said he had "an important proposal to make", namely that one of the empty rooms should be turned into a small chapel, that there should be a regular morning service, quite short, and Hugh should take it. It was a triumph of the "indirect approach" and a foretaste of similar incidents in parish life; for he was ever most pleased when some advance was initiated, not directly by himself, but by other often unexpected people. It was the more satisfactory in that now, in the year of 1928, he was looking ahead to the end of his time in Birmingham.

He had been asked to go back, perhaps on a married Secretary's salary, for a third year; but he was anxious to press on to his ordination, and had made his own plans, which were to enter Westcott House, Cambridge, for the Long Vacation Term, complete his course there by the following June, and spend the summer of 1929 in some well-paid interim job to enable him first to get married and then ordained in the autumn. The families on either side thought little of this proposal, and suggested that he aim at an earlier ordination and get settled into a curacy before taking a wife. Hugh's answer reveals his deepest beliefs both about marriage and about his vocation:

"Of course, to the ordinary person, that solution would seem the obvious one. I'm as certain as anything, however, that this is not the path God means us to take. The biggest thing about marriage is the complete fulfilment of each in the other. I don't believe we *are* our full selves before, do you? It is as our full selves, surely, that we wish to set out on our adventure in the service of God, especially when this 'adventure' is for the whole of this life, and for all time that comes after—for mere death cannot separate this Oneness.

It is my *full* self that I want to offer to God at my ordination, and that quite simply means ourselves together in the presence of God, even though it be *I* who is ordained into the ministry of the Church, yet mysteriously not the 'me' that I am now, for there will be you. But, of course, it is impossible to explain this to people; we must just work slowly for the removal of all difficulties, and not mind unexpected boulders in the path. . . . I think some day we shall be glad of our long time of preparation."

Two years of it were already over. In July 1928 Hugh left Birmingham, happy in the knowledge that "the S.C.M. has reached that interesting stage when all the sail is pretty well set to go ahead, the sympathies of most of the leading people in the University are with it, and my successor (from Mirfield) is exactly the right kind of person to carry the thing forward."

And so from Philosophy at Oxford, and Psychology at Birmingham, to Theology at Cambridge.

4

SET COURSE

Westcott House

It is a mistake to seek the True Church; rather one should seek for the Truth. Many have a devotion for the Truth, as they call it, and certainly not an equal devotion to Truth. . . . It is a comfort to me to think that all things, religion included, have to be made to square with God, and not He with them.

Life and Letters of Father Andrew

i

WESTCOTT HOUSE under Canon Cunningham was the obvious choice for one who was "always trying to fit things into a wider context" and felt it "a fatal thing for theological colleges" to be insular and isolated. "This," Hugh said to its present Principal, as he stood on the terrace with him the year before he died, "is the theological college in which I feel I can *breathe*!" It completed for him the process that had begun at Knutsford, and he felt for "the Professor", the inimitable "B.K.", the same respect and affection that he had felt for "the Chief". He admired, too, his wise and balanced welding into a "Common Life" of the varied elements and hues of church-manship that made up the House, and the catholicity that provided a different liturgy (Scottish, American, South African) for every weekday celebration. It was a catholic education in the true, not party, sense of the word, for

"B.K." held the ideal of "unity in diversity" to be fundamental to true Anglicanism.

Hugh's churchmanship had already undergone considerable change, and his St Aldate's friends might have thought that the pendulum had swung fully to the other side had they seen him now attending High Mass at Little St Mary's every Sunday morning. His contact with the Orthodox Church had taught him the value of Eucharistic worship. But his critical faculty was still active. Not that he was concerned about the minutiae of ceremonial which agitated some of his fellow-students. But he was not happy about the apparent dichotomy in Anglo-Catholic worship, which separates "Eucharist" from "Communion". The day of the Parish Communion had scarcely dawned which would be for him, as for many, the solution.

He consulted his Anglo-Catholic friends about these and other difficulties, but as he wrote of one of them, ". . . he couldn't give me the answers, because he admitted he had never even realized the questions!" He was discovering that the exclusive spirit and the closed mind were not all on one side, and that "Verbiles" were well matched by "Traditionalists". "Why do people think there is something sacrosanct about 'Tradition' as such? We should use Tradition as a *guide* to Truth; not put it *above* Truth. Some Traditions are good, some bad. We have to discriminate—in point of fact we *do*, or else we would all be R.C.s! The trouble is that catholic-minded people up to the present have had really only one mould to satisfy their needs. It is the tradition of mediaeval catholicism, and for want of a better they are going back to that, explaining away to their evangelical critics all the unsatisfactory elements while hanging on to what they feel is valuable. Of course we all make ridiculous mental reservations for the sake of what we value and love.

The old tradition-weighted forms and ceremonies come down to us through the centuries mellowed by the spirits of countless high and humble saints, and we worship God best somehow by means of them. And yet we must ride loose, I am certain. The question above all questions we must ask ourselves is 'IS IT TRUE?', not 'Does it help me?' We need not fear about the second question if we stand by the first." It is obvious that all the time he was "proving all things" in order to hold fast that which is good, and ruthlessly sifting out the fundamental from the controversial.

This critical objectivity and instinctive grasp of fundamentals is clearly seen in his comments on a lecture by an eminent psychologist to the Theological Christian Union on "Faith, Psychology and Healing", from which, he says, "I came away highly amused for I have never seen a crowd of theological students look *so* angry in unison before!"

The lecturer, after distinguishing between the "scientific" and the "priestly" mind, and challenging the "complexes" of the latter—suggesting sex-instinct, power phantasy, and desire for self-display as the underlying motives for ordination ("which made most of those present see, or look, red!") —had concluded, "Now spiritual healing may or may not be possible or true. No one is yet in a position to pronounce one way or the other. But in all discussion and thought, let the 'doctor' remember his unreasonable assumption that there is causal nexus everywhere and no mystery at all—and let the 'priest' recognize his predilection for the mysterious and marvellous—and both types make due allowances for themselves and their unconscious motives."

"I thought it a great pity," Hugh comments, "that he should have used manifestly bad logic to reach so admirable a conclusion. His whole speech was a perfect example of unphilosophical psychology—the kind of thing which puts

you and hosts of other people off 'psychology' (just as un-
reasonably, of course!) altogether. There was no time for
questions, or I should have asked him :

(1) If psychologists, too, were liable to complexes—such
as the assumption that all normal motives were bad
ones.

(2) If he would agree that power instincts, etc., were
neither good nor bad things *in themselves,* but could
be used and directed to either good or bad ends.

(3) If a psychologist lecturing to theological students
might not be indulging a power phantasy as much as
a parson in a pulpit!

"Seriously, though, this modern psychological attack on the
validity of religious experience is important; the argument,
I mean, that our judgment is warped by 'unconscious
motives'. Of course the argument cuts both ways! The
sceptic's judgment may also be warped (is, I believe) by an
unconscious motive—the hidden wish to rid the world of all
objective standards, including especially moral standards. I
have little patience with it therefore. However, in our time
the attack against religion is quite certainly coming from
that point, in a more subtle fashion no doubt. And yet I
can't find a book or a course of lectures on 'psychological
epistemology' *anywhere* (except perhaps Ward's *Psychological Principles*). It is time we woke up to the challenge,
surely."

There is so much here that is characteristic of Hugh. His
amused good humour when everyone else was furious; his
readiness to accept the gravamen of the charge ("so admirable a conclusion"); his detached fairness ("just as unreason-
ably, of course"); and then his neat turning of the tables.

Most characteristic of all is the final sentence. All his life he was quick to see the direction a challenge was coming from, and to grasp what was the essential position to be defended. More than that, his constant longing was to see the Church going in swiftly to the attack instead of coming up slowly to the defence. "Like a dog with a broken leg, our old Church lags a little behind with so many of the movements in men's minds today. Instead of joyously and adventurously running ahead, diving into the bushes of sex, barking and snapping at the cattle of industrial injustice, swimming out into the waters of destitution, with the assurance of the power to bring the wreckage back to land, and always coming back to lay itself at the feet of its Master for encouragement and commands to new ventures—we rather helplessly jog along, hanging back on the leash, a little afraid of trusting ourselves or our Master. The Church should have a POSITIVE message to give for every likely problem *before* it has taken hold on men's minds, and we Christians must watch the way things are moving and *anticipate* all along the line. If only the Church had been wise enough to do this before we were landed in this flood of sex-speculation, for instance. Stemming the tide isn't much good as a policy. The Church should be out in the field, proclaiming the far *greater* moral demands made upon men and women today by a positive ideal of chastity which is no longer based on fear of consequences. It's the same with Divorce. I have great sympathy with some of the 'reformers', but I hate their sycophantic appeals to Christian principles, when it's the spirit, the burning spirit, behind these principles that is really needed." How appropriate that twenty-five years later, at the height of his campaign against horror-comics and obscene literature, a Sunday paper should have dubbed him "the Church's watchdog"!

It is interesting to see the increasing awareness of what

his particular call would be, and to note the motive and spirit which determined it. Two letters are particularly revealing. The first, on a certain play then running in London :

"Of course it's a faithful study, but is the stage the place for a clinical demonstration? For a small proportion of men and women (doctors, parsons, schoolmasters, perhaps) their work demands the study of sex aberrations and sex psychology. Because one is dealing with aberrations the study is naturally not pleasant—pathology never is. But those whose responsibility it is to face this side of life, as a rule do so perfectly objectively, scientifically, wholesomely and stripped of shoddy emotion—as a doctor deals with a diseased body. It's a God-given vocation and responsibility, and one goes through with it in the spirit of service to Him . . . and to men and women for whom the battle has been too hard. But this is totally different from the present fashion in plays and novels, which I think will eventually commit suicide through sheer boredom and satiety."

The second, on a newspaper article :

"Do you ever feel like taking the bit between your teeth? I was reading a highly coloured article yesterday, describing the awful condition of certain parts of Paris. Had I not known from things I have myself seen there, I should have dismissed it as an emotional piece of journalism; but making allowances for that, and thinking it over in the light of the little I *have* seen, I just felt like going straight out there after ordination, and spending our time working amongst those English and American girls (art students, many of them)— *living* among them rather, going right into the heart of their haunts, and helping them by ordinary common friendship. . . . If parish life falls to our lot I want to go all out for this aspect of modern life—try to understand it, get at the roots of it, strip it of all the glittering tinsel and then show it to people in its ugliness and emptiness against the background of true ideas about themselves, about God and about *Home*. In concentrating on *that* point we shall be going to the heart of the Gospel one is ordained to preach, since it is *all* to do with the Incarnation."

And then, very characteristic of Hugh: "The trouble is, people don't associate bathing costumes with the Incarnation —that's the tragedy, and our life's job, as I see it."

A month later he tells how "two admirable lectures to us ordinands this week on 'Rescue and Preventive Work' (what a title!) by the Miss Hickson[1] (*sic*) who is in charge of the Archbishops' Committee, have been helping me to come to some definite conclusions. We must write a book (badly needed by the way) one day: a really constructive, positive work, on the family, limitation, sublimation, 'equality' of sexes, and so on. There is nothing bold enough, which carries the battle into the enemies' country, psychological and medical, as well as stark Christianity. There!"

All these things would be "one day". Meanwhile "if parish life falls to our lot . . ." there was much to be learned. The lectures on Sunday-school work and child psychology he found "immensely interesting and invaluable for us poor men who know so little about children and how the different ages should be treated"; an unduly modest estimate for the Pied Piper!

There was also practise in preaching. During his first sermon at a small church outside Cambridge "a Westcott man fell asleep, but he politely put it down to having kept

[1] Miss J. E. Higson, O.B.E.; see her book, *The Story of a Beginning*.

a 'vigil' turn from 3.0-3.30 a.m. and not to the sermon. One will never know!" The text, it is interesting to discover, was "He built his house upon a rock". Did he remember this first attempt when, a quarter of a century later, he took the same parable as the text for his sermon on Christian Marriage in Westminster Abbey?

Besides teaching and preaching, "we had an awfully interesting talk on sick visiting, by the Chaplain of Barts. It all makes me feel very inadequate, somehow, for the responsibility, and yet I think I'm going to love it best of all." Many of his letters at this time are on the subject of suffering:

"That remark you quoted about 'shallow people who have religious convictions and aren't worried by suffering' puzzled me awfully. I have thought it over and over again in my quiet times in chapel. I think it is that word 'worry' that is wrong. Religious convictions shouldn't deaden our *sensitiveness* to suffering: quite the reverse. It seems to me that if we are to grow like God we must, as St Paul says, learn to 'suffer with Him', which means surely, being tremendously sensitive to suffering, especially other people's. One who would, *because* of his religious convictions (experience, rather) agonize with men and women, and God, in their pain and suffering—feel it as his own and because he just couldn't help it—yet who all the time, through his vicarious suffering or in his own pain, was able to rest in unswerving confidence and with inner peace on the simple faith that in Jesus God somehow destroyed the seeming contradiction, literally and finally, by Himself suffering as one of us—I feel such a man would be very near the mind of Christ—my ideal of a Christian. There is all the difference in the world between *feeling* the sting of pain, so that it cuts right into one's soul, and the attitude which secretly denies that there can be anything *beyond* pain. It is this hopelessness which we mean by 'worry'; going round in circles of our own making instead of in a spiral widening out to the infinity of Love."

ii

Another man than Hugh might have found much justification for worrying in this most difficult year, the last of his long training and nearly as long engagement. How, for instance, was he to divide his very limited vacation periods between the conflicting claims on his affections! Lovers' meetings had often to be sacrificed to the necessity of earning money for the future, but he was naturally desirous of seizing any likely opportunity. But there was his mother (whose health was causing him deep concern) and his father, retired at last and settled in England, both longing to make up the lost time of years of separation. And there was the fascinating attraction of watching young John grow up. And, of course, there was the Bank—his boyhood's home; all these competing for his rare spells of leisure between college and "jobs".

Memory recalls some happy visits to Hoddesdon; musical evenings, with Uncle Clem singing his charming light tenor songs and Hugh pretending to scandalize the aunts with "Three for Jack" ("If you can't be true to one or two, You're much better off with three!"); or games evenings, playing Aunt Ethel's favourite acrostics, with Hugh wangling to get a word beginning with A and ending with M, so that he could win hands down with Anti-Disestablishmentarianism (*"twelve* syllables, please!"). But few children brought up away from their parents realize as Hugh did the heart-burning involved, or are so devotedly loyal to all concerned. Loyalty was one of his strongest and finest traits, and a long engagement gave plenty of scope for its exercise. Young couples who consulted him in later years about their several family tensions used to marvel at his insight and wisdom. There was little he did not understand of their predicaments, and he gave them of the fruits of his own experience.

Then there was the financial strain. He was no longer earning a salary but living on the last instalment of his ordination grant, out of which he was desperately trying to save every penny he could for what he called his Ideal Home Account. "I find I can manage it for 7/6d. return," he wrote, planning a meeting at a friend's wedding in London. "No, I'm not starving myself! I've only added *one* supper to the price I got for a de luxe edition of Scott (a school prize, I think)."

He was quite determined that the year 1929 should see him married. "Next September must really see us set off together on our work; and next two terms I shall try to do without fires in my room, be *very* careful what books I buy, and have my Sunday suit 'expanded' to last till I get my clericals. Hankies and socks I can wash myself, and anything else I can take off my laundry bill. And I'll let you know the result!" The result was a mild sensation in the college. Not only did he succeed in having no "extra laundry" charges on his bill, but held the record for being able to claim a refund on the basic rate! B.K. was touched, and managed to procure him a rebate also on the last term's fees, allowing him to go down early, as soon as examinations were finished, so as to spend June and July in a remunerative job. "When a man is getting married every little helps, doesn't it?" he said kindly—and unexpectedly, for he was not commonly sympathetic to engagements among ordinands. But Hugh had done his best to convince him that marriage can be a vocation as much as celibacy.

Earning money seemed even more difficult than saving it, and Hugh's search for holiday jobs proved as frustrating as had his attempts to work his passage from Oxford to Africa. He had a shot at journalism and "I've had two perfectly charming 'Editor regrets' already, and I'm thinking of buying a special album to keep them all in!" Amusing, in view of his future success in that field; but not amusing then, though he remained wonderfully hopeful and imperturbable even when both families asked him *what* he proposed to get married on and criticized all his plans as unpractical. "The more I tell people about all the plans and attempts I'm making, the more hopelessly unpractical I seem to become in their eyes," he wrote in an unusual—almost unique—outburst. "Is it *so* sinful after all to be hopeful? to hope that one of the 23 applications of various kinds I have made (12 more within the last three days) will give me the post I want?"

But they proved no more yielding than the editors. And frustration seemed likely to come, too, from another quarter, for it was proving difficult to find a vicar who would take on a married deacon, even if he did succeed in earning enough within the next three months to get married in the autumn.

The time came when Hugh wrote: "It is wrong, I suppose, to set one's heart on a thing *so much* that one can't see any other way. Having done our utmost on the practical side, the whole thing leaves our hands, I believe, and we must follow where the Spirit leads."

A year before, when he had first formulated his plan, he had written: "What happens then is not in our hands. We can be quite sure that if we do what is right between now and then, the right thing will be opened up for us. I think we must be careful not to try to guide God's hand to suit our wishes, but be ready for anything He may show us to do. I think there is always a risk of planning too far into the future and losing one's Faith, don't you? It's an Adventure, after all." Once again, as when he had written to his family in Africa, "It's disappointing, but we must make the best of it and things will work out all right", suddenly the way opened. At the last minute it appeared that things *were* going to "work out all right", and he was free to do full justice to his G.O.E. papers, especially, as might be expected, the one on Moral Theology. Whatever view the examiners took of his opinions on the more controversial subjects, they could not deny an *alpha* to his reasoning. He had not been W. D. Ross's pupil for nothing.

iii

It was the offer of a curacy that first changed the picture. The Revd J. W. Woodhouse,[1] Vicar of Christ Church, Luton, was losing his junior curate—a very live wire—and asked B.K., his former Principal, if he had a suitable man to replace him. "I have," was the reply, "but there's a snag." Jack Woodhouse had been a Student Mover, and his beautiful and gifted wife was an old student of Lady Margaret Hall. They had both been on the memorable Swanwick walk to Wingate Manor, where they, too, had been the target of one of John Maud's limericks. They were prepared to risk the snag. It was settled that Hugh should be ordained in Christ Church in the autumn, and in early June he went down to Luton to be introduced to the church and parish. "Fancy," he wrote afterwards, "you saying *you* felt

[1] The late Bishop of Thetford.

small as you sat in Christ Church last Sunday. It would be nothing to what I was feeling, daring to stand in front of all those people as one who was going to try to help them know Christ better. I think it must be nearly impossible for anyone brought up in a clerical family to know the fearfulness of mind and spirit which ordination means to one for whom it is absolutely foreign country, and who has no atom of right to presume on so high a calling, as I realize every day now." This was no natural diffidence. Hugh had plenty of self-confidence and, as a young man, his full share of Scots pride. His humility, which deepened as he grew older, came from the increasing dedication of all his gifts to the service of God.

He had obtained a post for the remainder of the summer term on the staff of a small preparatory school on which a sidelight is thrown in a letter to his future sister-in-law, then also teaching in a junior school:

"As one school-marm to another, preparatory though we be, and fellow sufferers, I daily relish your jokes and stories more thoroughly. I could not have believed so much humour and so few humans might ever be found together. Modern educational ideas and childish innocence both leave this world for the realm of Platonic Ideas, to be gazed at through a glass darkly. You in your small corner, and I in mine. . . . There is, for instance, Miss G. who invites me to tea five miles away, tomorrow afternoon, my 'free' one (2.45 to 5 p.m.). 'I say, Warner,' chirps my C.O. after pre-breakfast Early Work, 'you might take V . . . (son of a millionaire) to London tomorrow in your free time. He has many clothes to be tried on at the tailor's and his brother's tutor refuses to take him' (sound fellow). 'You will be able to catch the 4.20 back and be in time for prep.' Shaking him warmly by the hand, I express my utter astonishment that he should have put it as a question at all (except prefixed, perhaps, by 'nonne'—'expecting the answer Yes'). A hasty p.c. to Miss G.—and that's that.

"Yes, we shall have much to discuss and compare. But I wouldn't have missed the experience for anything. Seeing is believing!"

After that, Hugh was relieved to go back to private tutoring, this time at the Yorkshire shooting-lodge of a wealthy Irish racehorse owner.

"You would have been tickled if you could have peeped into the dining-room last night between 8 and 9. The family are away for a day or two (leaving me in charge of the boy), and I was all dressed up and sitting in splendid isolation at the head of a beautiful big polished table, with four great silver candlesticks. Hovering around me was the butler in full regalia of tails, and the first footman whose uniform was decked with brass buttons behind and in front, stamped with the family's Irish crest. As course followed course, I was offered in succession sherry, gin and soda, whisky, tonic water, ginger beer, kummel, benedictine and curacoa. After serving each course the men retired and waited on the other side of the closed door for the tinkle of a tiny silver bell at my elbow. Sitting there alone in the four-power candlelight eating a gorgeous peach and sipping port, I almost shamed the servants by laughing out loud, so absurd and grotesque did such luxury for me, of all people, appear!"

The humour of the situation was enhanced for him by the contrast of the "Ideal Home" which his bride and Jack Woodhouse, busily house-hunting in Luton, had at last secured. It was flanked on one side by a sweetshop whose bell tinkled ceaselessly all day, confronted over the street by a fish and chip bar which did a roaring business in the evenings, and overshadowed at the back by a large cocoa factory whose sickly smell hung heavily on the air in rainy weather. There he proposed to spend a week of quiet before the wedding, with a bed, a chair, a table and a fountain pen; scrubbing, cleaning, staining floors, and writing his ordination thesis on Spiritual Healing. "I should like some quiet away from people after these queer days up here, to get straightened out. I don't want to be all 'rushed' in my inside, and it will mean a lot to be able to browse (I can borrow books from Jack) and think and pray quietly in preparation for the wedding and ordination and a new life altogether. I only wish you didn't have to be all rushed with preparations, presents, etc.—but isn't it *wonderful* the way they are tumbling in?" It *was* wonderful. There seemed to be nothing needed for a home, from a piano to a nutmeg-grater, that had not been provided, to dumbfound those who had asked "what he proposed to get married on?" Even the wealthy Irishman sent him a handsome cheque (in addition to his fee), and offered to procure him a living in Ireland whenever he should want one!

iv

On 19 September 1929, Hugh was married in the Church of St Mary de Haura at Shoreham-by-Sea. The clerical friends and relations who were to officiate were astonished to find themselves rounded up a full hour before the service, and coached in every detail. "A remarkable young bridegroom," said one of them, the bride's old school chaplain, amused but rather impressed. "He knew exactly what he wanted, and he just put us all through it!" He would always be particular about the details of services, and he was determined to have his own wedding—the 1928 service followed by a simple choral Eucharist—just the way he wanted it. Even the Broxbourne relations had been practising Merbecke for the occasion.

The honeymoon was spent in Oxford—mostly on the river and visiting old haunts, including the University Church, where F. R. Barry, now the Rector, was preaching. It was Michaelmas, and he preached on Angels; those glimpses, as he called them, of the unseen reality, the "moments" at which the other world breaks through into this. "Queer chap!" remarked a Balliol don, coming out of church. "One often wonders just what he is getting at." It was perfectly clear to the newly wed couple, and they went round to the Chief's house to tell him so. "My dear!" exclaimed F.R.B. to his fiancée who came into the room just then, "I'm told I've preached a very honeymoonish sermon!" It seemed right that *he* should have preached it. "I owe more to him," Hugh had written only a month or two previously, "than to any one single person (except B.K.)."

The holy angels played a recurrent part in the marriage begun that Michaelmas. Succeeding Michaelmas-tides were marked by significant moments, both of joy and sorrow; especially sorrow, but those, too, were the moments when the other world breaks through.

From that fortnight of golden September days Hugh went into his ordination retreat, conducted by the Bishop of London (Winnington-Ingram), and on the Octave of Michaelmas, 6 October 1929, he was ordained deacon in Christ Church, Luton, by the Bishop of St Albans. The family were invited to lunch with Dr Furse afterwards. It was the first time he and Hugh's parents had met since the day, nearly twenty-seven years before, when he had visited them and their first baby in Umtali.

PART II
MINISTRY

5

NEW BEGINNING

Luton

"They that have used the office of a deacon well purchase to themselves . . . great boldness in the faith which is in Christ Jesus."

1 Tim. 3. 13. (Epistle for "The Ordering of Deacons".)

HUGH WARNER could hardly have begun his ministry in a better parish than Christ Church, Luton, in the days of "Jack" Woodhouse. The pendulum which had swung between St Aldate's at Oxford and Little St Mary's at Cambridge came to rest very happily at Christ Church, which occupied a position in Luton midway between the evangelical church of St Mary's and the Anglo-Catholic St Saviour's. A well-attended Mattins at 11 was preceded at 10 by a congregational Choral Eucharist at which there was a steadily growing number of regular, and especially young, communicants; while for Evensong one had to go early to be sure of one's favourite seat. Every possible organization flourished, led by a remarkable band of devoted workers. "Query," Hugh had written when first offered the curacy, "Is Christ Church almost *too* thriving?" He was not looking for an easy job. But as the junior member of a large staff he was to find no shortage of work, and to learn some useful lessons of teamwork in a live parish.

Mr Woodhouse's own gift was undoubtedly with the

young, and there was a vital and enthusiastic "Boys' and Girls' Own", in which Hugh met a different type from the student population of either Oxford or Birmingham; the young people of the Luton factories and the large secondary modern schools. His predecessor, a sort of Sir Galahad among curates, had captured their imagination and banded them into a romantic kind of crusade, but Hugh wisely decided that it was no use trying to imitate someone else's methods but better to plough his own furrow. He was given charge of the Scouts, among whom he was in his element, and after a few months the Vicar opened a new Sunday School in a hitherto untouched area, and put him in charge of a band of about fifteen young men and women teachers.

His visiting list was soon full, and there were clubs, classes or meetings to occupy most evenings of the week. But besides this he filled his odd moments and his weekly free day with extra-parochial activities. He did some lecturing for the W.E.A. He also joined the local Toc H and was speedily appointed Padré. Here he early demonstrated that deep concern for individuals which was such a notable feature of his ministry, so unswervingly befriending a gifted but wilful young man in serious trouble that he won for the Church a true penitent and eventually an ordinand.

Whether through Toc H, W.E.A. or other contacts, the new curate soon became known outside parochial circles as one whose Christianity was always ready for a challenge, and he found himself invited to an *avant garde* group of doctors who met to discuss Free Love and Emancipated Morals. After one or two encounters this group was surprised to find that it neither shocked nor scored over the exponent of an outdated morality! Hearing that they had invited Professor C. E. M. Joad, the great advocate of Sex Reform, to come down for a week-end, Hugh boldly fished for an invitation to the session. It was a memorable evening. Whether it was the smoke, the beer, or the subject matter, the young curate twice retired overcome by nausea : an expressive "acted parable" a Hebrew prophet could hardly have bettered. Each time he returned to the fray with renewed vigour, and by 2 a.m. he had ceased to be intimidated by the superior intellect or reputation of his adversary, for he had found one after his own heart—one who would "follow the wind of the argument wherever it leads" and face the crucial question, "Is it true?" As hormones and sex-starvation gave way to Josephus, Gospel sources, and evidences for the Resurrection, the group fell silent, feeling that a boxing match had unaccountably turned into a chess contest, and they could not follow the moves. They had hoped to see their champion knock the curate out. But Hugh, returning home in the small hours of the morning, declared, "That man will be a Christian one day : he is there already intellectually, but I suspect there are other than intellectual hurdles in the way." It was his first and last encounter with the Professor, but none could have said a more heartfelt *Laus Deo* over his *Recovery of Belief.*

What Jack Woodhouse made of these excursions is problematical, but he was a lenient vicar, and never one to clip his curates' wings. There were occasions, however, when he protested against too many all-night sittings. Hugh had been ordained priest on St Thomas's Day, 21 December 1930, in St Albans Abbey, and a few weeks later he wrote to his wife, away on a visit to her mother, "Your amusing disquisition on Nurses comes timely, for I've been having a try at the art, inasmuch as it is combined naturally (as I believe) with the office of priest." He had spent two nights sitting up with a woman dying of cancer, "but when I went to breakfast at the Vicarage, Jack didn't seem to approve of my being up two nights running, and said he always told the family to go to bed. I pointed out that that was just what I *had* done, and had stayed to let them do so. But E. has agreed to my plan now of visiting her at 1 a.m. instead of spending the whole night there, so last night I got to bed at 10 and set the alarm. It was queer going through the frosty empty streets at that hour. Her young sister was getting frightened, so I sent her down to the kitchen to make some hot bread and milk, and then fed E. myself with a teaspoon. She took it quite well and wouldn't let me leave the room, poor soul. So I stayed by her, praying quietly, till 7.30 when it was my turn for the Early Celebration." How much of this is "the office of a Priest", and how much is Hugh Warner?

Another letter, giving a full account of a fairly typical day, concludes, ". . . H. and G." (Oxford contemporaries) "seem to be going up in the world, don't they? But give me a simple parish. I *love it*." The letter is headed "Home, Surgery Hour". Early in his ministry Hugh, taking a leaf out of the doctor's book, instituted a definite "surgery hour" (6.30 to 7 p.m.) during which he made a set rule that he would be at home to any who wished to see him. It proved to be an institution of absolutely priceless value, and he kept it up throughout most of his life as a parish priest.

It was not very long after his "priesting" that the curate-in-charge of St Peter's, the small daughter-church, was offered a living, and after some deliberation Mr Woodhouse put Hugh in charge in his place. It was a bold and generous move, for he had been a very short time in Orders; but it was justified in the event, since when his call came to a living at an extremely early age, he had already had experience of a charge.

Enthusiastically he went ahead. A church, he decided,

should be "seen to be a Church", and as St Peter's was not much more than what would now be called a "pre-fab", with no spire to attract attention, he suggested to the local gas company that they might advertise the possibilities of gas flood-lighting! But St Peter's was soon "seen to be a Church" in a more lively manner. A collection of about sixty to eighty boys and girls were organized into a "Young People's Own"—a Bible Class, with their own cricket, rugger, hockey and indoor games clubs, their own Youth Council and weekly discussion evening, and a corporate Communion one Sunday each month, preceded by an *agape* or supper in the vestry on the Friday night. A box was provided in the church for requests for intercessions, sermon topics and the like. The place hummed with bazaar preparations, lantern services, story half-hours in the Children's Corner; and a Men's Fellowship was formed to discuss, at the weekly "smoking evenings", all the things that Hugh had found men discussing in Toc H and elsewhere: War and Disarmament; Sex and Marriage; Science and Religion; the Ethics of Business.

His vicar gave him a free hand, and when criticized by someone for seldom visiting St Peter's, replied promptly that he played full-back, not forward, and was ready to butt in if the game was hard-pressed. So far he had not been needed!

In February 1932 the "forward" asked for relief. Would the vicar preach for him at Evensong on the 21st, as he would like to be at home to welcome his first baby? "My dear boy," retorted Jack, who already had three children, "when you know as much as I do, you will know that babies never come on the day expected: they are always early or late—sometimes by weeks!"

On Sunday, 21 February, at the hour of Evensong, the

baby duly arrived. ("Next time," said Jack, "I'll take your word for it!") Hugh had been released from duty, as there had been a long and trying labour. "Young man," said the doctor, "in future I shall take you with me on my rounds!" Not knowing Hugh's interest in "doctoring", he had not expected such an objective approach. It was a firm tenet of Hugh's that the father should be present at the birth of his child. When the last number of the *Marriage Guidance Bulletin* before his death arrived, he was told that it carried a leading article by a doctor advocating this revolution in British custom. (Continental countries, of course, take it for granted.) He was very weak by then, but he opened his eyes wide at this and commented, "So I should jolly well think! About time!"

If ever there was a born father it was Hugh. The nurse, having hurt her hand one day, gave him the baby to bath and dress, and was astonished at his expert performance! It is amusing to remember that he had once declared he didn't think he would ever have a family. But he had doubtless long forgotten that.

He was not given much time to bask in his new status. Sunday night had brought him his first son; Monday morning brought his first living. It was to a speechless young mother, barely awakened from a well-earned sleep, that he read the astounding letter:

BISHOPTHORPE, YORK.

February 21, 1932.

DEAR MR WARNER,

I have to appoint a Vicar of our own parish of Bishopthorpe and in the course of my enquiries several names have been put before me, including your own. I am not yet in a position to make a definite offer, but I should very much like the chance of talking over with you the matter of work here, if you are ready to let me consider you further in connexion with the vacancy. I very much hope you will be willing for this.

Of course it is not a great urban parish, but it gives plenty of scope. The population is now 900 and is growing steadily. We specially need to make an impression on the young folk. There are several wholesome activities in the village, inluding a W.E.A. Tutorial Class.

I hope the new Vicar will be ready to act as my chaplain in certain ways—especially in arranging the Chapel for celebrations of Holy Communion, and helping me at them, and taking service when I have to be away. But of course this is always conditional on there being no service in the church at the same time.

Our traditions are very central. As regards externals we have an Eastward position, two candles, coloured stoles and frontals; choral celebration once a month. This suits the people here admirably. It would be a great mistake to introduce vestments or to stop the monthly choral celebration. The house is charming, but very likely too large and the village is quite prepared to see it let or sold.

The question then is—will you let me talk it over with you on the understanding that neither of us would be committed? If so, I hope you would come here for a night, to see both of us and the place? Of course we should like your wife to come too, but I understand that this would probably be impossible at the moment.

I most eagerly hope you will say Yes to this much anyhow!

Yours sincerely,
WILLIAM EBOR:

Mr. Woodhouse knows I am writing.

It *was* impossible for his wife to go too; it was difficult even to feel enthusiastic at that juncture about a move, a vicarage and a new parish, and there would be no friends or relations in the North. But Hugh's amazed delight was infectious, and although he dutifully consulted his vicar it was with little intention of listening very seriously to doubts about the wisdom of so early a promotion. It was his dear "Chief" F. R. Barry, he discovered, who had sponsored him; and what more, after all, could he learn from Jack Woodhouse, playing "full-back" down at Christ Church, that he could not learn under the eye of his long-admired and revered William Temple, whose visit to Oxford in 1923 had decided the course of his life? As he quite frankly told the Archbishop when he went up to see the parish, meet the churchwardens and be "vetted" by the Palace, "It isn't so much the parish that attracts me. It is the opportunity of being associated with yourself."

He spent the night at Bishopthorpe, and in the drawing-room after dinner the Archbishop motioned him to take a seat with "What sort of chair do you like, Warner? High or low." "You don't catch me that way, Archbishop," replied Hugh promptly. "Central, please!" The Archbishop laughed his enormous laugh and decided he liked the young man, but suggested that if he did become his chaplain it might be as well to conform to the custom of the diocese and address him as "Your Grace" rather than "Archbishop". ("Conform to the custom of the diocese!" chuckled Hugh, when repeating this at home. "Did you ever hear such a gentle way of ticking anybody off?")

The following day Dr Temple wrote to the Bishop of St Albans:

BISHOPTHORPE, YORK.

March 5, 1932.

MY DEAR MIKE,

Warner has just been here, and has seen some of the leading parishioners. I have made him the definite offer of the benefice, and we all very much hope he will be able to accept it. To me it seems that he has been sent to us to meet our exact needs—but I could not press that on you or on him. The population is growing, and we need to make an impression on the young. I believe he would have a better chance than most of doing that.

Of course the question is whether it can be right to leave a district of 5,000, with the advantage, at his age, of a vicar's supervision, for a benefice and parish of 1,000. But I gather from Woodhouse that he hardly could stay where he is much longer without an increase of stipend. There is very decidedly a whole-time job here—and no one can do more. And though I can't do much to steer him, I suppose that having the diocesan in his parish makes some difference in giving a young man someone to turn to.

I like him much, and should hope to see a lot of him, if he comes, and even though that must be destructive of anyone's soul, I might stimulate his wits!

Seriously, I don't want to give a wrong tip to the balance of his judgment, but I eagerly hope he will come to us. I think he can do what we need, and I hope we can do something to overcome the manifest drawbacks. But he will consult you, and will not settle in a hurry.

Yours affectly,

WILLIAM EBOR:

Hugh consulted his bishop, as he had his vicar, but the

result was really a foregone conclusion. As for settling in a hurry, the dates on Dr Temple's letters show that Hugh had wasted no time in writing his acceptance.

BISHOPTHORPE, YORK.

March 9, 1932.

MY DEAR WARNER,

With all my heart I thank God for your decision. I believe that you can do a splendid bit of work for Him and His Church in Bishopthorpe. And I am sure that you and I can help each other a great deal in our work and thought. I am looking forward immensely to your coming. Please tell your wife that the warmest possible welcome awaits her.

My spring and summer programme is extremely full. Do you think Monday, May 23, is likely to be a suitable day for your Institution? . . . If so I will book it, and shall be very glad.

God bless you and your work.

Yours very sincerely,

WILLIAM EBOR:

Oriel College VIII, 1923.

"Jack" Woodhouse with his curates at Luton.

Hugh Warner at Bishopthorpe.

6

DEVELOPMENT

Bishopthorpe

Wherever you find the nature of mind answering your mind, there you have satisfaction.

William Temple : *Nature, Man, and God*

i

THE new Vicar's induction was not without incident, and Jack Woodhouse, who was present at it, took back an entertaining account to the sick wife left behind with the new baby in Luton. It appeared that Hugh had rung the bell energetically ten times and had then found his feet leaving the ground as he rose up with the bell-rope. Being rescued—one version said by the intervention and superior weight of the Archbishop—he had proceeded, typically, to give it five pulls more. "That's ten years as vicar, and another five as Archbishop," commented the village. At the "get-together" in the village hall afterwards the Archbishop remarked that whereas he had intended to welcome the new vicar among them, he thought that "perhaps we should rather congratulate ourselves on having him still with us"!

The new parish was as different from Christ Church with its fairly homogeneous factory population as any parish could be. On the one hand there was "the village" with its feudal division into the Big Houses, who occupied the front pews in church, and the farms, market gardens and cottages, many of them having some connection, past or present, with "t'Palace", and all fully persuaded that Bishopthorpe was the hub of the universe. On the other hand, there were "those uppish new villa folk", as a very old villager tartly and most unfairly described them, who occupied the new housing estate growing up around the village as a business dormitory for York. It was a challenging sort of parish to run, especially for one who made it clear that he had every intention of running it on a democratic and not a feudal basis. Indeed, had he not stepped down from among the Big Houses by selling the old vicarage and going to live in a house in the village street? "Never mind," said one of the Mothers' Union members, "I *like* a poor parson myself. I think he understands *us*." Which was a consoling remark in view of the first M.U. committee meeting. The chief subject under discussion appeared to be "who should give the ham". The previous vicar's wife had obviously been the proper sort who gave whole hams for Christmas parties, and paid the members' fares on summer outings. How could one compete? Eventually Mrs Temple "gave the ham". It was not the only time her tact and understanding came to the rescue and saved the situation. But these things that so agitated the over-anxious, unwell, and untried vicar's wife daunted the new vicar hardly at all. He was far too busy, as always, making plans and making friends.

"Ee, he has such a *happy* face," exclaimed an old Yorkshirewoman, "I just love looking at it. I wonder how he comes to look so happy." "Perhaps," was the teasing reply, "he is happily married!" "Do you think so, my dear? Maybe so; but tell me, how did 'ee ever come to catch him?"

In many ways this was one of the happiest periods of Hugh's life, and a letter dated "Valentine's Day, 1933", when he had been in Bishopthorpe not quite a year, reveals him still bubbling over with almost schoolboyish surprise and delight at finding himself a husband, father, vicar and chaplain to his revered Archbishop.

"The sun is pouring in at my study window, and the birds are singing and mating, the garden looks lovely bathed in sunshine, and I can see dear old Daff grinning at me from his pram. The smile is meant for you, I think. Enjoy the sun, and the rest with darling Little Mum" (his pet name for his mother-in-law) "and don't feel you must hurry back.

"I had two more men at my Confirmation class. Quite a company it was. But Mrs N. and Mrs M. have had a row! Poor Mrs N. in tears here this morning, and says she is withdrawing her boy from the Confirmation class if Mrs M.'s son continues to come. Cheery, isn't it?

"P.P.C. Meeting last night. Just at the end Mrs S. got up and said, 'Please, Mr Chairman, on *what* system are the hymns chosen?' Whereupon everyone suddenly came to life (it was 10.30) and echoed, 'Hear, hear!' Mrs Temple grinned; and I thought, 'Now then, up and at 'em. . . .' Whereon they listened in amazement to (a) that we had to choose 12 hymns every Sunday, (b) we worked to a list of 'known' hymns, supplied by Stanley,[1] (c) we *never* give them more than one new hymn on any Sunday, (d) we choose Hymns—

(1) according to the Lessons
(2)   ,,   ,, ,, day
(3)   ,,   ,, ,, sermon
(4)   ,,   ,, ,, topics in the newspapers.

Miss A. suggested congregational practice, at which I leapt

[1] Stanley Johnson, the organist.
The "known" hymn list was very limited, as the late Vicar had only recently changed over from *A. & M.* to *English Hymnal*.

with joy and told them I should have them once a month and expect every one of them to be present. (Laughter.)

"Mrs Temple thought it might be a good plan to have a new hymn repeated more often, so that the congregation could get to know them as well as the choir. 'My husband found he had to do this when he met opposition to the English Hymnal in London.'

"They all went home happier and wiser people; albeit convinced that crossword puzzles are no longer fashionable if the same excitement can be got out of 'spotting the reason'!

"It was all very merry, unlike similar debates elsewhere! So go ahead and choose the list for next Sunday, and have some new ones they have already had four or five times. And they'd love 'Sun of my soul', I'm sure.

"Well, well, how I do go on (as Little Mum, bless her, would say)!

"His grace the Lord Archbishop of York, Metropolitan of England, will send his chauffeur and automobile to meet the wife of the Vicar of Bishopthorpe on Thursday next at 4.45 (is it?), if she will condescend to ride in so abject a carrier.

"Och! how I *love* you. There! Your own husband and proud father of David Hugh."

"It was all very merry." "Ee, he has such a *happy* face!" "He really likes people, doesn't he?" There was the secret of Hugh's dealings with his Church Council, and with the whole of the parish. He was so completely good-humoured, and he believed in taking them into his confidence—especially about church services. If he would never delegate the choice of hymns to any organist it was because he was chiefly concerned to make church worship sincere and intelligent, and he knew how a suitably chosen hymn can drive home, and an unsuitable one short-circuit or dissipate the effect of a sermon or the theme of a service. For the same reason he made great use of the 1928 Prayer Book, with its more modern and intelligible language, but again, not without first consulting his P.C.C. At his first Council meeting, at which those present had, for the most part, expressed their appreciation of the new Bidding at Mattins and the prayers he had used the previous Sunday, one cautious young Yorkshireman had burst out, "It's all right *so far*. But what I want to know is, where is it going to end?" "With the 1928 Prayer Book," replied Hugh promptly, and patiently explained his position. But when the meeting was over he singled out the young man to walk home with, to make sure that his reasonable doubts were fairly met and allayed. The man became one of his warmest supporters.

Hugh explained his position again in an answer he gave once to a visiting preacher of the "Traditionalist" school, who criticized these modern deviations from the language of our incomparable Prayer Book. "But it is I," he protested, "who am in the *true* Prayer Book tradition. The whole idea of those who compiled it was worship in the vulgar tongue, and a language understanded of the people. Elizabethan English has long since ceased to be *that*. If you had lived in Cranmer's days you would have abhorred his incomparable Prayer Book as an innovation, and have been arguing for the retention of Latin!"

One other innovation, if so it can be called, was his occasional transposition of the place in the service of sermon and prayers. He remembered the American students who had looked upon the prayers as a formal exercise preliminary to the main point of the service—the preaching. They were members of Protestant sects, but were Anglicans very different? "The Church of England has been more concerned

to exhort people to pray than to teach them how to do it,"
so had run one of the questions in his ordination exam. He
was determined not to be content with exhortation, and
whenever he preached (as he often did) on the subject of
Prayer, he gave the sermon after the Third Collect, and followed it up with carefully prepared meditations or intercessions that put the teaching into practice. He had already
discovered, in this connection, the power of the small group
with a special concern; and a most valuable legacy from the
previous incumbent was the "Fellowship of Prayer" which
met every Monday night to pray for the needs of the parish
and in particular for any who were sick or in trouble. In his
small band of Sunday-school teachers also he had a firm and
loyal group who learned to worship and pray together, and
would have strongly refuted the critic who protested, "I
don't want someone who looks about 19 to teach me how to
say my prayers. I've been saying my prayers all my life!"
(But that was when Hugh had based a Lenten course on
Bede Frost's *Art of Mental Prayer,* without stopping, in
his youthful enthusiasm, to consider how far it was above
the heads of a village congregation.)

If there were things the new vicar could teach his parish,
there were some the parish could teach him; as, for instance,
that you cannot fix the date of Harvest Thanksgiving (however anxious you may be to book a good preacher well ahead)
until you know when the harvest is likely to be in! A simple
proposition that had not occurred to the ex-curate of Luton,
where the harvest is hats and Vauxhall cars. There are things
that really matter in the country. "A good sermon," remarked a parishioner coming out of church one Sunday.
"Yes, a good sermon, but" (chuckling over one of Hugh's
illustrations) "he was all wrong about they 'taties'!"

ii

Hugh Warner had much to learn about Yorkshire people and about village life, but he knew where he was with the young. "I think he has more chance than most to get hold of them," the Archbishop had written to Dr Furse. How he did so is indicated in a letter written some twenty years later by Mrs Temple: "I have just come back from a visit to Bishopthorpe, and it was moving to hear the younger generation talking of what they owed to Hugh. G. and M. (old Youth Club members now married) said, 'We always ask, "What would Mr Warner have said?" when we are arguing about anything.'"

When this was read to Hugh as he lay ill in hospital, with the comment, "It's nice to think one has done some good in one's life, isn't it?" he murmured, "Oh, I don't know; it was all very ordinary." "Ordinary" was not what the parish thought it when he set about establishing a "Young People's Own" on the Luton model. He was criticized for making "too much fuss" of the young people, caring more for them than for the old, and "asking for trouble" in running a mixed club of boys and girls. There were, naturally, the occasions when the critics were able to say, "I told you so," though one could have pointed out that such "trouble" was an immemorial feature of village life and not the responsibility of the Youth Club.

There were other times, too, when the Young People could be difficult. "Every one of my Y.P.O. committee has 're-signed' in the course of this winter," he remarked one evening. "And what do you do now?" "Oh, nothing! I never *accept* their resignations. It's just youthful exuberance. After all, they've got to learn. As far as that goes, not all grown-ups know how to give and take on committees." He could not always persuade grown-ups to take the same patient and tolerant view.

He was incurably optimistic where the young were concerned, and nothing if not persistent; and he had the approval and encouragement of the Archbishop, who gave up time to welcome and address a "Youth Conference" from Bishopthorpe and neighbouring parishes in his Palace grounds.

In one respect Hugh ventured to differ from His Grace, and that was in the formation of a Scout troop. The Archbishop was all for the Church Lads' Brigade, which he had seen functioning in his diocese of Manchester; but for Hugh, after twenty years of scouting, to become enthusiastic about C.L.B. methods would have been for the leopard to change his spots. "Fancy taking boys to camp and having Army cooks to cook for them!" he groaned, scenting again that silverside of salt beef. "Dear Arch! I must educate him!" It was the only subject on which he ever suggested educating his Archbishop! Whether or not he succeeded, Dr Temple realized that it was no good asking a man to do a job he could never put his heart into. He had given him the mandate to get hold of the young; he must do it in his own way.

As time went on he found that one of the great handicaps to work among the young was the lack of premises of their own. Behind the new vicarage were some old disused stables, and Hugh set to work, with the unskilled labour of his youthful helpers, to turn them into serviceable club rooms. For two days at St Andrew's-tide 1935 (the Patronal Festival) he sat out in the road in a sentry hut, warmed by a brazier, to collect gifts towards the cost of the rebuilding and decorating. The clubroom became rather a sore point at home: bits of furniture and pet belongings had a way of disappearing and turning up in the stables rather the worse for wear.

It must be admitted that this debonair attitude towards belongings, whether his own or other people's, was one of Hugh's weaknesses. But it was all in a good cause—the cause of his beloved Youth.

"Don't only talk about his youth work," wrote someone who had heard that his life was being written. "Be sure to say how wonderfully good he was to the sick and dying." As in Luton, he would sit up night after night with a dying parishioner, until once the Archbishop, like Jack Woodhouse, gently remonstrated with him and warned him that he must not allow himself to be imposed on. But the "imposition" came from his own heart. It was not only the dying of whom he was thinking, but of those who loved them; and often at the end, if the District Nurse was away in another village and could not be fetched at once, it was he who would lay out the body and attend to the various immediate and practical details that so distress the family in the first shock of bereavement. It was those whose sick he visited, whose sorrows he shared and whose loved ones he buried who most regretted his departure from Bishopthorpe.

He loved the old people of the village, and once gave an "Old Folks' Party" at the vicarage, inviting a member of his Y.P.O. committee to come as stenographer and take down for future preservation the various anecdotes they had to tell of life in old Bishopthorpe and of past vicars and Archbishops. Once they got the idea there was no stopping the flood of reminiscence! The party ended with community singing, with the young vicar, "who looked about 19" in the midst of all the "oldest inhabitants", their average age well over 80, bravely singing the old popular songs.

One old lady, a real "character", was not present that day. (It was she who, when asked if she felt equal to coming to the Mothers' Union Christmas Party at the Palace, had replied, "Aye, I'll coom if they send t'car for me." "They" did.) Hugh used to take her her Communion in her cottage, and at first was a little disconcerted at the way she would absent-mindedly stroll over to the fire and give the stew a stir. "Go on, luv," she would say, "I'm listening. It's luvely!" "I suppose it doesn't really matter," he said dubiously; "she is on such intimate terms with God that it all seems quite natural."

Hugh might have told the Archbishop that it was not the parish that attracted him, but once in charge he was not more capable of such detachment than a mother with her first baby. He put his whole heart into the job of a parish priest and took a real pride in the fact that each Christmas he took his Christmas card round personally to every single house in the parish; an intensive visiting operation known at home as "doing a hoosh".

It was still a reasonably small place, where the Vicar could know every inhabitant of whatever denominational allegiance. Thanks to "t'Palace" tradition, it was, in fact, predominantly Anglican, and all the children attended the "Archbishop of York's School" in the village. Christians of other persuasions for the most part worshipped at the local chapel, which had a long tradition of loyal membership; but Hugh was concerned about the Romans, scattered around the new villas, when he found in the course of his visiting that few of them seemed to be able to get into York to church. He offered to run a special Sunday bus to take them to Mass, a gesture which met with surprise and gratitude but little co-operation. Gradually he discovered that the lack of transport was often just an excuse; and almost without realizing it he found himself embarked on "Marriage Guidance" (though the phrase was unknown in those days), sorting out the religious and personal problems of "mixed" marriages.

In this connection it is not irrelevant to anticipate an incident which belongs to his Epsom days. A young Irish woman called at the Vicarage there asking to see "the Father". "This is the Anglican vicarage," she was told. "Isn't it the Roman priest you want?" "Och, no, the creature!" she exclaimed. "He's a good man, but what would he know about *my* troubles, and him a bachelor!"

That was when Hugh had already some reputation as a marriage counsellor; but among his Bishopthorpe flock his views were suspect. Not only did he run a mixed Youth Club, but he had even been known to mention Sex to his Confirmation candidates, and had given a couple who came to put up their banns a shocking book called *Right Marriage*. The young man's mother returned it to him with a letter saying what she thought of it, and one of his regular congregation decided to be married and put up the banns elsewhere. Preparation for marriage is now increasingly recognized (largely as a result of Hugh's own influence) as being as essential a duty for a parish priest as preparation for Confirmation; but a pioneer is seldom popular to begin with, even with those he is out to help. There *were* the encouragements, like the young couple who came to consult him, and in gratitude for his help and advice called their first baby "Hugh". But they came from York, not from the village.

He was learning the difference between ideals formed in the University or Theological College and the hard facts of a country parish. It was not only that his youth was a handicap; but he met for the first time here, and had not yet learned to take into account, the immense conservatism, prudishness and suspicion of new ideas which has to be reckoned with in the country. He discovered, for instance,

99

that the choir disliked singing Christina Rossetti's lovely carol "In the bleak midwinter" : verse 3 made them uncomfortable! A neighbouring vicar's wife, who had suggested to a mother in her village that, considering two of her daughters had illegitimate babies, she would do well to give the youngest some straight teaching, had been met with an indignant "Thank you! We never have any indecent conversation in our house." Such a mentality was not easily receptive of methods suited to Oxford, Swanwick and Birmingham, or for Toc H discussion groups in Luton. Perhaps that was one of the most valuable lessons that could have been learned at that stage. As he used to say in after days, "You have to start with people *where they are*."

iii

Parish life, with a rapidly growing population, was, as the Archbishop had written to Dr Furse "decidedly a full-time job"! But no more than in Luton could Hugh's activities be confined to parish boundaries. In November 1933 he was invited by the newly elected Sheriff of York, Mr H. L. Creer, to become Sheriff's chaplain, and was thus swept into the civic life of York with all its colourful processions and functions at Guildhall, Minster and Assize Court. The Sheriff was re-elected for a second term, and in March 1935 Hugh preached the Assize Sermon in the Minster.

Sitting by the Sheriff at the Assizes, hearing the Judge on circuit try cases of forgery, bigamy, rape, shoplifting and every conceivable form of crime, he learned much about legal procedure and also about human nature on both sides of the "Bar". It was an experience he valued greatly, as he did the friendships and contacts made at civic breakfasts and banquets.

Happy also were his contacts with ecclesiastical circles. On arrival there had been a formidable succession of "state calls" from the clergy and their wives of the Rural Deanery of Ainsty and of the Minster "Close". At some point during the tea-party the question would always be slipped in, as it were nonchalantly and "by the way", "Of course, you knew the Archbishop before you came, I suppose?" And the rather baffled surprise at the answer was always amusing. But the total lack of resentment or jealousy at the oddity of the new appointment (evidently one of Temple's aberrations!) and the extraordinary kindness of all the clerical neighbours was one of the most heart-warming features of those early days.

There was a strong family spirit among the clergy and their families of the scattered Ainsty Deanery, for the clerical Chapter met for early Communion at the different parish churches in rotation, followed by breakfast at the vicarage and a morning's discussion. There was some rivalry among the clergy wives over exciting breakfasts, and the discussions were stimulated by the seasoned experience of Harry Woollcombe, then Bishop of Whitby and Rector of Bolton Percy, and the powerful intellect of Canon A. E. Baker. Hugh derived considerable mental stimulus from him, as also from speakers who came out from York to address his Youth Study Circles or newly formed C.E.M.S., such as Dean Bate from York Minster, and Dr James Welch, afterwards Director of Religious Broadcasting and at that time Principal of St John's Training College.

But, best of all, Dr Temple was at this time writing his Gifford Lectures, *Nature, Man, and God,* and asked his chaplain to compile the index, a notable fulfilment of his promise to Dr Furse to stimulate the young man's wits. Here was the "new wineskin" Hugh had been looking for at Cambridge, when deploring that Catholicism so far had only been able to find a mediaeval mould. A liberal Catholicism, said Temple, must look forward, not back. The mediaeval synthesis was no adequate answer to the Marxist dialectic, the great modern challenge to the Christian Faith.

As he sat in his study surrounded with the galley-proofs Hugh had the same sensation he had experienced when he first heard William Temple speak at Oxford, the sudden clarity of hearing one's own tentative thoughts put into lucid and convincing words. Once, visiting in the village, he had been amused at the remark of an intelligent agnostic : "I never thought Christianity merited serious consideration, but when I find men like you and the Archbishop believing in it, I suppose I must think again." "You and the Archbishop" seemed to him an incongruous bracketing of a brilliant master with a humble disciple. Nevertheless, their minds had this in common, that they moved, albeit on different levels and at a different pace, in the same direction. The combination of surrender with integrity, the balance of heart and head, which shines through Hugh's letters from Oxford and Westcott House, receives its classic expression in the second chapter of Temple's Gifford Lectures. When someone complained that the tension there demanded was psychologically impossible—or at least extremely difficult for the ordinary person—Dr Temple simply smiled and said, "But it must *be* possible, if God is Truth"; and then, quoting his favourite Browning, "On the earth the broken arcs, in the heaven a perfect round." It was that serene and enlightened faith that won Hugh's firm allegiance.

There were other qualities, too, which the Archbishop and his chaplain had in common : an imperturbably equable temper, complete fearlessness of public opinion, a strong sense of the comic, and an essential simplicity and lack of self-consciousness. "Weren't you nervous, preaching in front of the Archbishop?" a kindly parishioner asked the new very youthful-looking vicar. "I never even thought of it," he answered. "After all" (with a twinkle), "I've been preaching in front of God for the last two years." It was a perfectly sincere answer which the Archbishop himself would have appreciated. He, too, was no respecter of persons. The close contact with Dr Temple was Hugh's constant joy and inspiration, whether it was his own daily visit to the Palace to take Mattins, or the Archbishop's visits to the parish church where he always celebrated on Sundays and read the Lessons at Evensong if at home, and regularly preached on Christmas morning and Easter evening. Once Hugh asked him to take a preparation service for Christmas Communion. He willingly agreed, and was far less upset than his chaplain to find the congregation consisting of four people—two from the Palace and two from the vicarage! His feelings on this subject can be gauged from the following letter:

Feb. 8, 1934.

My DEAR WARNER,

The Magazine announces that there will be no service on Ash Wednesday apart from the early celebration. I know the difficulty of getting substitutes when you are preaching for someone who cannot just exchange with you. But I expect there are some people who would be sorry to have no service that evening, and, as I happen to be free, I would gladly take an evening service with a short address if you like to arrange this and to announce it on Sunday. Do as you think well about it, and please remember that as far as I am concerned, I am just as happy doing it for six people as for sixty or six hundred—so don't let that influence you. But if you think it better to leave things alone, those who wish can no doubt go to the Minster.

Yours very sincerely,

WILLIAM EBOR:

The highlight of Hugh's chaplaincy to Dr Temple was, of course, the Coronation in 1937. Looking back on those six years in Bishopthorpe, they seem to have been punctuated by Royal occasions: the Jubilee celebrations, the passing of King George V, the Abdication of Edward VIII. The Abdication was a sad time for Hugh. Like all Toc H men he had loved and admired the Prince of Wales, and he was greatly distressed, not least by the revulsion of feeling among his parishioners against the idol who had let them down. No one who knew Hugh or his convictions about marriage could doubt what were his views on the matter, and a large congregation at Evensong on the Sunday following doubtless expected to hear them elaborated. What they got was a sermon on the text "Judge not, that ye be not judged".

That was completely in character. He was always able to distinguish between actions and motives, between principles and people. Over and over again, in sermons, in press articles, and in his last book, he tried to drive home the point that we must never hesitate to call certain actions "wrong", but we must always hesitate before calling those who do them "bad". It was this distinction—learned long ago from W. D. Ross in Oxford, and observed throughout his ministry—that Sir Alan Herbert (in his book, *The Right to Marry*) characterized as "pleasing, but puzzling". The world always finds the Christian combination of conviction and charity "puzzling"; and accuses the Church alternately of harshness and hypocrisy; for a pagan society, it has been said, cannot forgive, it can only condone or condemn.

The Archbishop of York and his Chaplains
in their Coronation robes, 1937.

As Vicar of Epsom, with Civic Authorities.

As Vicar of Epsom, with the Grasshoppers Club.

Launching the "Education for Marriage Campaign"
at Birmingham, 1953.

(Birmingham Post and M

Hugh had regularly accompanied the Archbishop as his cross-bearer at services in the Minster and at meetings of Convocation in St William's College; but as the Coronation drew near he wondered if there were not more important people who should fill this rôle on such an occasion. "I shall quite understand," he said to Dr Temple, "if you choose someone else for your chaplain for the Coronation, and I shan't mind." "Oh, you won't, won't you?" said His Grace quizzically. "Well," said Hugh honestly, "I suppose I should really; but——" "I should just think you would!" was the reply. And so it was that the two children (there was a second boy by now, the Archbishop's godson, named Andrew after the village church) sat in the study and listened to the commentator announce, "Now there enters a purple figure bearing the Cross of York". "Daddy! Daddy!" exclaimed the elder excitedly. Later he was taken to the cinema in York to see the Coronation film. Alas! the purple figure bearing the Cross of York was cut off abruptly just below the shoulders!

Hugh's letters home describing the rehearsals for the ceremony were full of entertaining anecdotes:

"After the rehearsal today, when we were all back in the annexe and were being told through a loud speaker what we had done wrong, one of the funniest incidents happened that I have ever seen. The Voice said, 'And also the canopy must be removed immediately after the Anointing of the Queen. Today it was kept there all the time.' Then a little voice which could be heard all over[1] said conversationally to the announcer, 'Yes, but of course that was the Archbishop's fault.' We all smiled with great glee at the uncensored *sotto-voce* remark on the loud speaker. Then suddenly we noticed

[1] Note Yorkshire-ism!

Cosmo charging through the crowd in his full rig-out, looking like thunder, but—this was the funny part—charging towards the loud speaker, only to find that the man at the microphone wasn't there at all—he was right over on the opposite side of the building! You should have heard William retailing this story to Mrs T. at lunch afterwards. His laugh shook Lollard's Tower!"

His comments on the day itself were characteristic. "The Creed impressed me very much. As I listened to it I thought —how grand if all who listened truly meant it." "Rather wish we could all have said Our Father together instead of listening to it being sung." "In the Veni Creator I happened to look at the two young Princesses and saw them look at each other and smile at the words 'Give peace at home'— bless them!"

He was deeply moved by the whole service, and especially by the beauty and simple sincerity of the Queen. Years later, at the new Queen's coronation, as he sat at home following the service in the vellum-bound service book he had kept from the former occasion, he was really seeing the last coronation and living it over again; and his prayers were especially for the Queen Mother, for whom it must all have been so poignant. Somehow that was like Hugh, who instinctively picked out the one person in any gathering who was feeling lonely or for whom it was difficult.

iv

In 1938 the tiny parish of Acaster Malbis was added to the living of Bishopthorpe, and Hugh, with the help of his newly purchased cyc-auto (known to the Y.P.O. as "Mr

Warner's chatterbang"), gave up one day a week to visiting there, anxious that the smaller parish should not feel neglected. About this time, too, the Archbishop appointed him Sub-Warden of the Lay Readers in York Archdeaconry; he was also Director of Clerical Studies in the Ainsty Deanery.

Free time was becoming more and more scarce and precious. A note in the parish magazine to the effect that in future the vicar would consider Friday his "free day" merely brought more people to the vicarage. "I see you are free today, and I knew I'd find you in," was one visitor's greeting. It was difficult to think of the right answer. The best chance of recreation and one much to Hugh's taste, was a visit to the Repertory Theatre in York, where Phyllis Calvert was then leading lady. Edward Waddy, the leading actor, worshipped regularly in Bishopthorpe Church, and undertook the coaching and production of a parish Passion play— "The Upper Room"—himself playing the part of Judas. Two of the more conservative parishioners who disapproved of "plays in church" undertook to stand at the church door and show people into their seats, though they could not bring themselves to stay and see the performance. The vicar respected their opinions, as they respected his.

As for holidays, they generally took the form of a week in camp with the Scouts and "locum" duty in remote country parishes. There were also occasional visits to the relations in the South, and two important family events during these years completed Hugh's happiness. His brother Cyril had decided to be ordained, and his mother, having now two sons in Anglican orders, had at last come over to her husband's Church and had been confirmed. Hugh, more than anyone else in the family, after all the letters they had exchanged in his Oxford days, knew and appreciated what the decision had meant. He knew how deeply she had always cared for family unity.

v

Meanwhile Hugh's devoted work for Youth was bringing him into ever-widening circles of Church life, and it was with great enthusiasm and excitement that he returned home one January day in 1935 from a conference at Swanwick called together by the Youth Committee of the Church of England Missionary Council. As at Nyborg Strand nine years previously, the need had been clear for someone to give a wise and energetic lead to the enthusiastic but irresponsible youthful elements. Who first conceived the idea on this occasion is not remembered, but certainly Hugh was one of twelve who felt the concern and who, at the eleventh hour of a conference that was not going too happily, met in a certain room X one night to pray about it. Their prayers, heart-searchings and discussions, which went on past midnight, proved the birth-throes of the new Central Youth Council, of which one of the twelve, Tom Craske, now Bishop of Gibraltar, was the first Secretary, and of which Archbishop Temple promptly agreed to become Chairman. Another of the twelve, who became first chairman of the executive, was Canon Roland Roberts, at that time Diocesan Missioner in Guildford Diocese. Whatever Hugh's contribution had been to the thought and prayer of that meeting in Room X, as to subsequent meetings of the Council ("and I would say without hesitation," Tom Craske has asserted, "that Hugh's was easily the most creative mind among us"), Canon Roberts was sufficiently impressed to recommend him as a Missioner when the Epsom Deanery in his Diocese of Guildford planned to hold a Mission in 1938.

He had already taken both Retreats and Missions in the York Diocese, but this one proved a milestone. The *Guildford Diocesan Gazette,* commenting upon it, remarked that

"One of the most encouraging reports comes from the parish of Walton-on-the-Hill. This parish has a large number of wealthy residents, many of whom are there only at week-ends. Obviously there had been very careful preparation, and considerable imagination was shown in planning three gatherings at the beginning of the Mission. On the Saturday afternoon there was a well-attended drawing-room meeting; on the Monday evening a large social gathering for the whole parish, organized by the Mothers' Union, and later the same evening another social gathering for members and friends at the British Legion headquarters. Because of these preliminary gatherings, the mission services did not start until the Tuesday, but when they did the church was crowded each evening. In addition there was a cinema service for children in church each night at 6 o'clock, and at this the attendance grew gradually until there were over 100 present. On the second Sunday there was a parish Eucharist at 9 o'clock with 70 communicants. All this is most encouraging when the size of the village is taken into consideration. The Rector concludes his Report by saying that 'the appeal throughout was to the will and the understanding rather than the emotions. We owe a great debt of gratitude to Mr Warner, a man with an unusual combination of gifts . . . who has not spared himself, and has radiated the Divine Love among us."

Hugh's personality leaps from every sentence of that report; the careful and imaginative planning, the success with the children, the use of films, the starting with people where they are, in wealthy drawing-room, parish hall, or

British Legion; the appeal to the understanding ("Is it True?"); the leading up to the parish Eucharist; the tireless energy, and the impact of one who "really loves people". People in Walton still talk about that Mission. They were talking about it so much in that summer of 1938 that when the Vicar of St Martin's, Epsom, Canon Pattison Muir, resigned his living through ill-health, Canon Roberts suggested Mr Warner's name to Bishop Macmillan as his successor.

The Bishop's letter offering him the living came during a holiday "locum" in Kirby Underdale, a small village in the Yorkshire wolds, memorable chiefly for having Calor gas in the vicarage and Lord Halifax, then Foreign Secretary, in the congregation. Hugh immediately wrote to the Archbishop, also on holiday, and received a reply to the effect that, while not wishing to influence him one way or the other, he had rather hoped he might stay a few years longer in Bishopthorpe "to establish your ethos". Meanwhile another letter came from Farnham suggesting that we should go down for a night to see the parish and the Bishop and talk things over. Hugh wrote to the Archbishop that we were going on the following Monday, to which Dr Temple returned the answer, "It looks black for Bishopthorpe".

Bishop Macmillan often recalled "the day you drove down to Farnham". It was August Bank Holiday; trains were problematical and Kirby Underdale some miles from a station. Hugh decided, on the rash impulse of the moment, to drive all the way. He had only recently acquired a car, and never driven further than from Bishopthorpe to Kirby Underdale. However, it was a glorious day, and he sped down the Great North Road until, at Kingston-on-Thames at tea-time, he ran into a tight Bank Holiday traffic jam on the bridge, and was nearly mown down by a fire engine. Hungry, hot, exhausted, and more than a little giddy, we drew up at Farnham Castle *very* late in the day, to find the Bishop and Mrs Macmillan standing on the front doorstep exclaiming with relief, "*Here* they are!" Never would we forget their kindness and the warmth of their welcome—nor the sleepless night that followed while Hugh still giddily drove a car and the claims of Bishopthorpe and Epsom did battle in his mind.

From the first he had felt that Epsom was a true call, and his chance to tackle a really big job of work. Moreover, he would be nearer London for his Central Youth Council, near to good schools for the three boys (Francis had by now arrived), and within easier reach of our parents as they grew older. Only the personal feelings of loyalty and affection for Dr Temple made him hesitate; but not for long, for he knew the break would have to come some time, and even if he did not leave Bishopthorpe it was quite possible that the Archbishop would one day go to Canterbury.

The visit to Epsom the following day clinched the matter. By the time he arrived back in Yorkshire the decision had been made, and when he returned from his holiday the news was out. Many parishioners echoed the sentiment, "it looks black for Bishopthorpe", though none with quite such a Yorkshire "backhander" as the member of the Sanctuary Guild who exclaimed, "I hate all changes; they are always for the worse—at least, all I've known have been so far, and I expect this will be no different!" Among the regrets at leaving just then was the fact that we had at last begun building a permanent vicarage, and had even persuaded an amenable architect to adopt most of our own ideas and suggestions. Hugh always loved plans of any kind. His common answer to the stock question, "A penny for your thoughts," was generally, "Just plans!" He was as ready to plan a new house as anything else.

Like the original welcome in the village hall, the farewell had its touch of humour, for the parish had decided on a grandfather clock for its parting present, and there seemed to be nowhere to "house" it until the day except at the vicarage. Having stood there for a week, it was smuggled under cover of darkness into the vicarage car and down to the village hall to be suitably "presented" by the Archbishop, as a great surprise, in the course of the evening. In his speech of thanks Hugh told the parish (and the Archbishop heard for the first time) the story of his undergraduate doubts, and how it was due to that visit of Dr Temple's to Oxford that he had ever been ordained, to become their parish priest.

When he went for the last time to the Palace, Dr Temple called him into his study. "Kneel down," he said, and putting his hand on his head gave him his blessing, and appointed him his honorary and permanent "personal" chaplain. So the link was not to be broken after all, and it was still in the same capacity that Hugh attended him at his enthronement when he was afterwards translated to Canterbury.

7

GATHERING IMPETUS

Epsom

Of (*fifty*) years he seemed; and well might last
To (*fifty*) more, but that he lived too fast . . .
Yet, had his aspect nothing of severe,
But such a face as promised his sincere . . .
With eloquence innate his tongue was armed:
Though harsh the precept, yet the preacher charmed.

John Dryden: *Character of a Good Parson*

i

"THE Greeks had a word for it," wrote the Vicar of Epsom in his parish magazine, appealing for some church cause; "*acedia,* spiritual inertia. Perhaps surprisingly Christian moralists used to include it among the seven deadly sins. We won't call it by so harsh a name—let us call it just 'waiting for the vicar to ask'. I beg the laity to see the Church as 'their show'. I pray for a volcanic awakening of initiative, an earthquake to release the latent goodwill, a daily explosion of practical service as each need of humanity passes before our conscience."

The sin of *acedia* had little chance to flourish in Epsom during Hugh Warner's incumbency of St Martin's. To see each need of humanity passing before their conscience the parishioners had only to read their monthly magazine, which became known as unique in the diocese. As soon as he had known that he was to leave Bishopthorpe, Hugh's mind had leaped ahead "making plans", the first of which was concerned with the transformation of the magazine from the conventional parochial news-sheet into a potent instrument of evangelism. As usual he was quick off the mark. He was instituted in December 1938, and in January 1939 "No. 1, vol. 1 (new issue)" appeared in a fresh cover, as simple, arresting and different as a born impresario could devise. The artistic etching in the centre, of St Martin on horseback dividing his cloak with the beggar, was drawn by the Reverend E. S. Dorling, who had recently designed the arms for the newly created borough of Epsom and Ewell; and the motto "Naked and ye clothed me" epitomized the theme of its contents for the next twelve years, the love of Christ expressed in the service of men.

The contents were as arresting as the cover. Besides the forceful Vicar's letter there was a wealth of teaching (and humour) in the "Answers to correspondents"; not to mention the general knowledge quizzes:

"How to score (out of 45 questions):

45 is excellent,
40 nothing to be ashamed about,
35 pretty poor,
30 Well, well, well, well!
25 (or less)—What about joining one of our Study Groups?"

The things that "every instructed layman ought to know", ranged from digests of Canon Law or the Lambeth Encyclical to practical details of local housing; while the *un*-instructed layman would be accosted by a disarming "Broadsheet for non-churchgoers", and topics such as "The Church's Challenge to Communism" (how like Hugh to put it that way round!).

As time went on prose and verse contributions came in from parishioners; but the most popular feature was the inimitable "Vicar's Diary", which often ran into several pages. During the lean years of paper shortage the number of pages was strictly rationed; but Hugh simply published a four-page "supplement", went into smaller print, announced that the price would remain the same, the material would be more varied than ever, and the circulation must be stepped up. When eventually he turned over the editing of *St Martin's Gazette* to Thora Wallis Myers (now Editor of *The Guider*), he had definitely, in Dr Temple's phrase, established his ethos.

Three aspects of that "ethos" especially stand out from a perusal of these records. The first is the typical balance; seen in the equal emphasis on worship and on Christian citizenship, and often in the presentation of both sides of a controversial question. The second is his ever-ready championship of the under-dogs, the awkward cases, the unpopular minorities. The third is his constant habit of being two jumps ahead; as he had written in his Westcott House days, "The Church should anticipate problems *before* they get a hold on men's minds."

All three characteristics are apparent in the letter written five months before war broke out, urging people to weigh seriously what should be a Christian's duty in the event of war. Having put the case fairly and cogently both for Pacifism and for National Service, he ends : "My own judgment is clear; but I recognize that my judgment may be wrong. Believing it to be right, I would be belying my own advice if I did not use this opportunity of publicly supporting the movement for National Service. I do not intend to argue about it, as I don't suppose my judgment is sufficiently important. But I do plead that whichever class of possible Christian opinion you feel is right, you do not sit idle, but *work* for the cause which is for you Christ's cause." Of Hugh's dedicated energy during the war years what could not be told! Nevertheless, fifteen months later he is leaping to the defence of the conscientious objectors, publishing a short story by one of them in the *Gazette*, and upholding their right to their position against offended members of the congregation.

"Who is my neighbour?" As the years go on the answer can be studied in the pages of the *Gazette* as it records Hugh's successive "concerns", nearly all unpopular causes for which he was not content merely to take up the pen, but in most cases initiated or sponsored some remarkable practical experiment, whether it was running a pig-farm for the unemployed (1939, his first project almost from the moment he arrived in Epsom), opening a school for refugee children staffed by older refugees, on church premises (1940); lending a room in the Church House to the Jews for a synagogue (1941); inaugurating a Marriage Guidance Council in the borough, with a good deal of sniping from a section of the Borough Council and Press (1945); or shocking a neighbouring borough into an overdue piece of slum clearance (1949).

It was in the *Gazette* that Hugh developed his flair for journalism. He knew that it went into countless homes that never heard a sermon, and he looked on it as the supreme opportunity to proclaim to the man-in-the-street and outside the pew what Christianity really is, in theory and practice.

ii

In August 1939, the Central Youth Council,[1] on which Hugh had succeeded Tom Craske as secretary in 1938, sent him as one of the British delegates to the Oecumenical Youth Conference at Amsterdam. His fellow-delegate was David Say, who succeeded him as secretary of the Church of Eng-

[1] The Central Youth Council became the Church of England Youth Council in 1942.

land Youth Council, and afterwards became the first secretary of the British Council of Churches.

Of "Amsterdam" Hugh wrote in his book, *Christian Youth Leadership in Clubs and Youth Centres*, after painting a characteristically vivid picture of the assembly:

"Few of those present were not conscious that their common allegiance to Christ as Saviour and 'Victor' had made of a multi-coloured crowd one organic fellowship. The unity there experienced was felt as a given reality into which each entered, and which remained after all had returned by ship, rail and air to their respective homes.

What to some may have seemed a theory was here demonstrated as a fact. It will not be so difficult to believe, therefore, that the further characteristic of the Christian Church, which has always been central to the whole conception, is also true. The Love of God is not a phenomenon of this world, but an eternal fact (or it could not be God's). Death is for the Christian a gateway, not a cul-de-sac. The fellowship of those who find their unity based on their response to the love of God extends beyond the grave. . . . We go therefore, as leaders, to youth exasperated and disillusioned by the failure of so many experiments to create new social orders, with the reality of the Universal Church extending throughout this world and on into the next—a Church both militant and triumphant."

True to this vision of the Universal Church, Hugh invited Dr Nicolas Zernov, an ardent labourer for genuine Reunion, to preach from his pulpit and to speak to a group of parishioners. He always valued his contact with the Orthodox Church, whose conception of worship so profoundly affected his own, with its vital awareness of the Risen and Ascended Christ and the life of Fellowship in the Spirit, where Western devotion tends to concentrate on his Death and Passion and the individual's response. To the end he kept up his membership of the Fellowship of St Alban and St Sergius, and read its quarterly organ *Sobornost* (palely translated "Fellowship").

Christian Youth Leadership was published in January 1942. Hugh had been succeeded as Secretary by David Say in 1940, and was now Chairman of the Executive Committee. His capacity for swift and easy writing was one of his greatest contributions to the work of the Council, as indeed was his swiftness of leadership in general. "Spiritual Quislings" he had entitled an article in the *Central Youth Council Review* in 1940. "I mean those who betray the cause from within. You know them—the committee members who think that the monthly social and the Saturday hike is the Christian's answer to the Devil's blitzkreig; or the Diocesan Council member who says, 'Well, let's put that on the agenda for our next quarterly meeting' instead of going all out *at once*." "I want to secure," he wrote elsewhere, "that in the minds of those who one day will have to rebuild society there is NOW implanted a full Christian set of convictions."

"At once": "NOW." These were key-words with Hugh, with the result that here, too, he was apt to be two jumps ahead of the rest. There would be a discussion as to how to co-operate with non-Christian youth clubs, or how to commend the work to local authorities under the Government's "Service of Youth" scheme, launched shortly after the outbreak of war. "I've got something written on those lines," Hugh would say quietly, after listening for a while to the discussion. "Here are the first three chapters. . . ." Some found this disconcerting. They wanted longer to consider their policy. But Tom Craske consistently encouraged him.

"If you are not ready to put this out as the Council's publication," he would say, "then let Hugh go ahead and take the responsibility. He is quite willing!" Consequently Hugh's spate of books, pamphlets and "manifestoes" soon held the field, and he became known as an "authority" on Youth. He was always a little surprised at this himself, and once remarked, "It seems to me one only has to take an interest in some bit of Church work that has been neglected to be considered an 'expert' "—a discovery he was to make again later on in the field of sex and marriage.

In his first publication, *Youth in Action* (1939), when still Vicar of Bishopthorpe, he had as editor collected a remarkable number of "experts" to write on their own particular subject in relation to youth work. Now in *Christian Youth Leadership* (1942) Hugh wrote directly from his own experience in the practical field of parish life. What has been noted as the weakness of his sermons proved an asset in his publications, namely, that he wasted no time on "grooming". "Dear old chap!" he said once of a colleague, "he's a perfectionist! If I took all that time over a bit of writing I'd never get it into the Press at the psychological moment." Miss E. M. Jeal, who acted as his most devoted voluntary secretary all through his Epsom years, tells how he came into his study one morning and at one sitting dictated "straight out of his head" a pamphlet on *Parochial Youth Fellowships and how to Plan them in Wartime,* which thereupon went immediately through the press without a single correction or alteration. He had only put into direct words what he was already putting into action.

Similarly an appendix to *Christian Youth Leadership* describes the most remarkable of Hugh's many clubroom enterprises, the "In and Out Club" at Epsom. Though launched officially as an experimental youth centre by the united action of Anglican and Free Churches in the borough, it reveals a familiar pattern, and one need not ask who it was who seized the chance of securing for a low rent the derelict shop in the very centre of the town, sat out on the pavement for a whole week with a tub to collect the necessary £300 for rent and furnishings, provided a nucleus of keen youth members to start the ball rolling, or enlisted a contingent of troops posted in the locality to distemper and repair walls and floors in their spare time. In the first nine months of the Centre's opening 200,000 entries had been made in the registers—most of them Service men. After a year the actual club membership stood at 600, of which 200 were nurses from local hospitals. The military police described it as the best run club known to them; and a letter from Canada declared that "I have heard the 'In and Out Club' spoken of with gratitude in N. Africa and in Italy. You little know what it meant to us all!" It should be noted that the club was inaugurated *before* the Ministry of Education had launched its "Service of Youth" scheme, so that no public funds had at first been available. Hugh, as usual, was well ahead of public opinion.

All this time he was doing much speaking, as well as writing, for the Youth Council, and was in demand all over the country to address meetings of youth leaders; an activity after his own heart, for he was always looking and planning ahead, and just as before the war he had tried to help the young to anticipate and face the Pacifist versus National Service challenge, so in the thick of the war years he always kept his eyes on what part youth would have to play in the future, and how the men and women of the Forces could be fully re-absorbed into parish life. His thirty-page booklet, *YOU, After the War?* published by the Churches' Committees for work among the men and women in the Forces, was distributed by the Chaplains' Department to every individual on demobilization. The last page is pure Warner:

"If you get home and find that things are not moving amongst church members, do not stand outside and fire criticism from the safe refuge of the crowd. Get busy yourself, start a discussion group on current problems, and decide what you and others in the Church ought to do about them."

Copies on the table at the back of his parish church had a notice affixed: "This booklet contains the general programme on which we are working at St Martin's."

iii

To describe in detail the programme on which we were working at St Martin's would be utterly impossible in the compass of one chapter. Hugh described it himself in his next book, *Christian Advance* (*1943*). He gave it the subtitle "Ideas and plans for local action". In *Christian Youth Leadership* one catches a glimpse of the Hugh Warner of Birmingham days. *Christian Advance* recalls the Oxford Study Secretary, as it describes the various cells with which the parish was honeycombed. During the first year of "phoney" war he had seized upon the enforced inactivity and boredom of A.R.P. and N.F.S. units to initiate study circles on the Christian Faith. His book describes ambitious syllabuses on doctrine, social problems, or citizenship, covered by business men, housewives, or youth groups. Gradually the whole parish became a graded school of religious education, from junior Sunday School to a hand-picked group, largely of university graduates, studying the knottiest of moral problems; and the mothers of the children in one of the schools in which he taught asked for a study circle for themselves, in order to keep up with, if not ahead of, their children.

A delightful description of Hugh's methods with his study groups comes from a member of one of the earliest ones:

"I can remember Hugh's great gift of teaching. He never laid down the law. He made us use our own brains. It was such fun learning from him! He made Christianity seem both hard and attractive. It was an all-out business with him, and perhaps that was the secret of his radiance and power. Once in Lent he asked us to think quietly of the most precious thing we possessed, and to thank God for it. And then he said, 'I wonder what you all thought of? For me it is knowing Jesus Christ.' Many times he brought home to us that a Christian is a mediator—a mediator of the sweetness of Jesus. And because of his strong conviction about that, he was able to look at and stand beside many situations which were sordid, or horrible or sinful, and bring the healing power of Christ to them. He expected us to do the same. There was always the positive action or spirit of Christ to bring to a situation, and he expected a Christian to try and do it. No self-pity—no complaints! That was the way he lived himself. 'Remember you're a Christian,' I heard him say one day, 'not a jelly-fish!'"

When *Christian Advance* was published, Hugh sent a copy to the original leader of the pioneer group who had then left Epsom and was doing good work in another diocese, saying, "I think it should have been dedicated to you, since you are responsible for so much of it." "The humility of it!" she comments, "thanking a beginner like myself, when really it was entirely due to his prodding and guidance that I got launched into church work at all.

always feel Hugh had a great sense of the potentiality of each parishioner or person he met, and he was able to help them to develop their talent—often almost pushing them into a job!"

Another group member put it thus: "In the early days of my knowing him I remember him looking round at a group of us (a seedy-looking collection of people I had been thinking), and saying in effect, 'Now *you* are the people on whom God is depending to go out and change this town,' and I thought, 'Does he really *mean* it? Surely he can't.' But he DID, and in time I came to see it too."

iv

It is tempting to linger over these glimpses of Hugh with his study groups. But all this hive of activity needs to be seen against the background of the "blitz", the black-out, the strain and stress of a parish on the direct air-route to London, and Hugh's intense personal care for every stricken home. Every day there were intercessions in church for those in the Forces; long lists of names, street by street, were published in the *Gazette* each month, and a copy was sent abroad to them all throughout the six years of war, with a personal letter full of cheery, chatty, local news at Christmas and other times.

Various units, some of home, some of Commonwealth troops, were successively posted in Epsom, and Hugh became the official chaplain. It was primarily for church parades that he had printed a *Simple Guide to Mattins and Evensong*. He remembered from Oxford days the outsider's criticism of difficult church services, and his point was proved by the rapid sale of his *Simple Guide* far beyond his own parish. During the war the population more than doubled as civil service, medical and other specialist groups moved from London out to Epsom. These, too, were welcomed into church life or study groups. Later came the flying bomb and rocket phase, when the process was reversed and Epsom children were evacuated in large numbers to Wales or the North country. To them also letters were cyclostyled—and what inimitable letters Hugh could write to children, generally adorned with comic little drawings—and some of their delightful replies would be printed in the *Gazette*.

For the victims of war, whether evacuees, refugees, or "bombed-out" families, his care was unceasing, and he expected the same of others. "He was always meeting needs," writes a parishioner, "with a great gift for improvization. He not only started the club for the Canadian soldiers, sensing their loneliness, but he encouraged all his churchpeople to open their homes to them and to share what they enjoyed of home life, and many of us did. When we had refugees among us he sought all sorts of necessities and comforts for them—and succeeded in persuading people to give them. I remember giving a bed—an act of rash generosity, as it wasn't long afterwards that we really needed it for ourselves—but Hugh gave himself so generously that one hardly stopped to consider with prudence when he showed one a need that could be met at one's hands. It was a spirit nearer to the life of the early Church than anything I have met before or since."

The same parishioner tells how he visited her one day when she had barely recovered from the birth of a new baby and was struggling with no domestic help and two other small children to care for. "He left me and came back within an hour with Ivy—a charming girl of 16, who stayed with me as mother's help for two or more years. And such help was practically unobtainable those days! Things like that just seemed to happen around him."

All this by day; and at night the air-raids. It became a kind of joke in the parish that the Vicar must have some personal contact in the Luftwaffe, he sensed so uncannily where a bomb was going to fall and was invariably on the spot before either doctor, air-raid wardens or rescue squad. Parishioners identified with pride the two-stroke engine of his "Chatter-bang" dashing off to the scene of action with the prompti-tude of a fire-engine, even before the sirens had ceased their alarm. Those who tell not only of his heroism but of his practical efficiency and resourcefulness are legion, including the matron of a maternity home that received a direct hit, who was still waiting anxiously for A.R.P. assistance when Hugh appeared and immediately took charge of the rescue of mothers and babies alike. But it was not his wont to be spectacular. It is the simple, even humorous anecdotes that describe him best; how when others were coping with the hysterical occupant of a damaged house Hugh would be found in a back room quietly feeding the baby; or the way in which at the height of the noise and damage he would cheerily pop his head into a house where he knew a couple of nervous maiden ladies would be shivering under the stairs. Patrolling the entire parish throughout the night raids, he soon discovered where lonely people were left in a house when the others were out on duty. "We got into the way of expecting him when it was a really bad night," said one, "and *what* a difference it made to us!"

He was sensitive, as always, to the personal aspect of things. "Have you arranged for 'clearing up' a house after a casualty?" he asked the air-raid wardens once. "People do it themselves," was the reply. "But you can't expect a wife to wash her husband's brains off the wall herself when a piece of shrapnel has gone right through his head and killed him. That happened last night." "I suppose not," said the warden, somewhat shaken; then, curiously, "Who *did* wash the walls?" "I did," said Hugh simply. He spoke little about such things at home, where his own "blitz" baby, Martin Michael, was born on one of the noisiest nights of all, at Michaelmastide, 1940. He arrived in the closely shuttered dining-room while the rest of the family slept in the reinforced cellar beneath, and was named, like the Bishopthorpe Andrew, after his father's church. "What shall we do," said Hugh, "if our next parish is All Saints?"

v

In this time of strain and stress Hugh was more concerned than ever that none should be able to say, "The Church tells us to pray but doesn't tell us how." He had a special St Martin's Prayer Card printed, *Everyday Private Prayers for the Home, the Church, the Train, the Countryside,* of a size to be carried in pocket or handbag, with a simple form of morning and evening prayers and suggested subjects for intercession. Similar help, both for adults and for young children, was given from time to time in the pages of the *Gazette,* and a special leaflet was printed for private use in air-raid shelters.

Among all his ceaseless activity, both of day and night, the essential ministry of a parish priest never became a matter of mere routine. His children recall a week in which he had taken an exceptional number of funerals (twenty a month was a low average), and one of them asked, "Daddy, don't you get *sick* of funerals?" His reply was illuminating: "I find something new in the service every time." So, too, he might have three or four weddings on a Saturday afternoon, but "every one is different", he would say. To the sacrament of Baptism he sought to restore its ancient dignity by administering it after the second lesson at Mattins or Evensong once a quarter (on "fifth" Sundays). Parents and godparents were deeply impressed by these christenings, though diehard parishioners would occasionally ring up the vicarage to inquire if it was "a proper service or those silly baptisms" that morning.

He had no intention of dislodging the much-loved and very well-attended Mattins (the "proper service"!) from its settled place in the tradition of the parish; but he laid increasing stress on the sung Eucharist that preceded it, and was always trying to train the "8 o'clock plain and 9.30 coloured" to appreciate each other's worship and grow together towards a parish Communion. He loved to celebrate a full festival service, with choir, music, vestments and procession in the very early morning of Ascension Day, but he was equally happy taking the one evening Communion of the year—a simple, deeply reverent celebration on Maunday Thursday. There was room in his truly catholic mind, as in the Anglican Church, for both.

Besides his stress on weekly Communion as the focus of parish life, he gave also a central place to the Parish Fellowship, and once greatly scandalized some good and regular communicants by pointing out that the two were complementary parts of Church membership, and that it was worse than pointless to kneel at the altar on Sunday side by side with those whom you showed no desire to meet or know on weekdays. "The Church is a family," he said, "and can you imagine a family in which the members scarcely know each other's names! We must not only pray together, we must play together." "I often saw him," one wrote, "looking round a gathering and smiling as though he saw in it the happy and glorious working of the Holy Spirit among us."

Others recall rather his dealings with individuals, particularly as a confessor (though he would never urge as "generally necessary to salvation" a medicine prescribed in the Prayer Book for certain conditions). "It was a very great thing," one writes, "to have the help of his tremendous Christianity allied to psychology; and that wonderful sense of stillness and inner calm gave confidence to the most timid."

Naturally the Vicar had his critics. There were those who resented any experiments with Church services; those, as in Bishopthorpe, who disliked the accent on youth; those who were suspicious of marriage guidance and shocked at his frankness about sex; and those who were even more suspicious of his politics! Epsom was a "true blue" citadel, but the Vicar was an admirer of Archbishop Temple! He declared himself ready to let his Church Hall to all (Christian) political parties and inculcated the Christian duty—not of voting a particular way but—of hearing all sides fairly and voting intelligently. Consequently each party strongly suspected him of favouring the other, just as in Church matters some thought him "High" and others "Low". If asked which he called himself, he twinkled and said, "Just a sane Christian!" But his integrity was patent to all, and he had a happy capacity for accepting criticism if useful, or discounting it if captious, but never resenting it as personal. In his favourite book of devotion, *The Spirit of St Francis de Sales*, the most heavily marked passages were those on a Christian acceptance of criticism.

vi

May 6th. To Bury St Edmunds for a "Religion and Life" Week. I stayed with the bachelor Provost, and realized with a shock how quiet a bachelor's house can be. ("From the Vicar's Diary", *St Martin's Gazette* for June 1944.)

"Canon of Guildford and Vicar of St Martin's, Epsom, is a manner of describing Hugh Warner," wrote a reporter who came to interview him some years later, "but it leaves such a great deal unsaid. It says nothing of the home life of a father, a mother, and a large assorted happy family—a sense of which is felt on entering the vicarage door." He must have had the usual tumultuous welcome. Certainly no one would describe Epsom vicarage as quiet, even without the nursery party. The telephone rang incessantly, so did the doorbell; the study knew little of the peace of a clerical sanctum; and "surgery hour" (expanding well beyond the hour in these days) often demanded the sacrifice of dining-room and drawing-room as well, where the children cheerfully entertained those waiting their turn.

In 1940, after Dunkirk, Hugh's mother-in-law, in her eightieth year, had been persuaded to leave her house on the South Coast and with her other daughter join the family in Epsom. "I came to stay with my son-in-law three years ago," she said to a Mothers' Union member, "and here I still am! What do you think of that?" "I think," was the frank reply, "that it speaks very well for you *both*!" Shortly after her fifth grandchild, Hugh's first daughter, was born in September 1943 she was taken ill, and by the time the flying bombs began to arrive in the following summer she was unable to be moved from her room, though the family were sleeping like sardines under the Morrison dining-table or under the stairs—all except Hugh, who dozed outside, fully dressed, in an already damaged and unsafe Anderson shelter, whence he could keep watch on where the "doodle-bugs" fell, and shoot off instantly to the scene of action. The lovely but unwieldy Queen Anne vicarage had been exchanged by now for a smaller house which lacked the protection of shutters and roomy cellar. After a near miss it became obvious that the children should be evacuated, and Hugh was left with serious sickness in the home and sorrow and danger all around in the parish.

For the many husbands and fathers experiencing the same loneliness he founded the "Grasshoppers' Club", which for some reason caught the imagination of the Press and was widely publicized. It began simply as a weekly get-together at the King's Head, to make sure of a good meal without the misery of cooking or washing up, and to encourage low spirits by cheerful companionship. Members then added interest to the evenings by talking on their jobs, their hobbies or subjects of specialized knowledge; other subjects and speakers were gradually brought in (hence the name, for the grass widowers hopped from topic to topic), with the result that long after families had returned and the war was over the Club continued as one of the most interesting, if informal, organizations in the parish, strengthening the already strong masculine element in the congregation.

"Little Mum" died at Michaelmas, and Hugh sent his sister-in-law off to join the family out of range of the deadly rockets and to recover from the long strain of nursing. So it was that, a few weeks later, he was sitting quite alone in an empty house when he heard the B.B.C. announcement of the sudden death of William Temple. Immediately he took train to Westgate to be of what help he could to Mrs Temple, and to look his last on the serene and ever-youthful face of his "dear Arch".

For the next three years all his spare time was devoted to compiling the *Daily Readings from William Temple*, which was published in 1948. It was a sheer thank-offering and labour of love; no attempt to compete with the many other memoirs, appreciations and estimates of the Archbishop's work and thought that came fast from the press, but simply a desire to share with others what William Temple's influence had meant to himself. "I always thought of him," wrote one parishioner, "as carrying on when Temple died"; and another, studying *Readings in St John's Gospel* for the first time, said, "I couldn't think why it all seemed so familiar; and then I realized it was Hugh's sermons in Epsom. How he must have been soaked in Temple!" When Hugh died, Mrs Temple commented on a sentence quoted in some of his obituary notices as specially characteristic of his teaching about marriage—"Oh, I *do* like that! What a nice saying of Hugh's!"—and was astonished to be reminded that its origin was a printed letter which William Temple gave to all engaged couples who asked him to marry them. It was no habit of slavish imitation. Sometimes he was almost unaware that he was quoting. He had absorbed William Temple's ideas for so long that his mind could not but continue to work in the same way.

In the *Gazette* he wrote of the Archbishop's death, "We all feel it hard to understand why it had to be. Can it be that, had he lived, we in the rank and file of the Church might have left too much for him to carry? Too often in conversation with our unbelieving friends have we pointed to "The Archbishop" in justification of the Church's relevance to daily life and quoted his writings. But the matter was not yet sufficiently in the heart of us ourselves. Our own witness lacked robustness so long as we leaned too much on him. Now he has blazed the trail. The Church of England is in the affection of thousands who before saw no vision there. It is left for us to be filled with his spirit, that his message of personal service of others and of love for members of other Christian denominations may ring out in cities, towns and villages with that authentic note of authority which was so truly his."

vii

The oecumenical vision was something Hugh had first caught from William Temple in his S.C.M. days, and no account of his Epsom ministry would be complete without some reference to his relations with other denominations. He seized every opportunity of co-operation with other Christian ministers and congregations in the borough, and on more than one occasion he managed to combine in a harmonious team elements whom it had been prophesied he "would never get to play".

In June 1944 the Epsom Council of Churches planned a Religion and Life Week, of which Hugh wrote in one of his letters to those in the Forces, "I can think of nothing which has so jolted the public of the borough into a live interest in the coming Religion and Life Week as the debate which took place in the Borough Council Chamber last month." An alderman had resisted the request of the churches for the use of the public park for meetings on the curious ground that if it was granted to Christian bodies it would have to be granted to Communists, as "there were more Communists than Christians in the borough"—a manifest absurdity, the animus of which was indicated by a further remark that "I can think for myself. I don't need parsons to tell me what to think." Gleefully Hugh took up the challenge, pointing out that the main purpose of a Religion and Life Week was to encourage, even goad, people to think for themselves. "It is precisely the closed mind that is so typical of many of our 'intellectuals' that the Church challenges."

And most of the speakers (a brilliant list) would not be parsons! "Had it not been for this debate there might have been some doubt of the necessity for holding a Religion and Life Week at such a time," proceeded Hugh. "But in fairness to the Council I ought to make clear that these views were not shared by the Majority. There were some very good speeches on the other side—in fact to those of us who were in the public gallery the debate brought out some of the wisest speeches which we have heard in the Council Chamber." It was this lively interest in civic matters, about which he was ever exhorting his flock to concern themselves, which was such a thorn in the flesh of the alderman, who publicly accused him of "getting at" Council members. "I challenge him," retorted Hugh cheerfully, "to produce his evidence for so ridiculous a statement!" For anyone who knew Hugh's direct and fearless approach it certainly was ridiculous to suggest that he would resort to lobbying and wire-pulling rather than the fresh air of the pulpit and press. But it was true that he had staunch friends and allies among the civic authorities, with whom his relations were in general peculiarly cordial.

Four years later a more intensive campaign, known as the "Christian Challenge", was launched, with Hugh Warner and John Blamey (the Methodist minister) as joint secretaries. For a full year beforehand there were street groups and study circles preparing for it, and the plan this time was to concentrate not so much on big meetings (generally packed by the already converted) as on visits of teams and speakers to schools, factories, clubs, house groups and other ready-made audiences. Of Hugh's part in this the Reverend John Blamey has modestly written, "As you know, Hugh and I were joint secretaries, but his leadership really provided the impetus for the whole thing. At the 'briefing' meetings held daily during the campaign his lively and dynamic leadership were much in evidence, and I know that Brian O'Gorman, our official leader (now at the Methodist Central Hall, Sheffield) had a very high regard for him." On the last day of the campaign the Baptist minister, in a spontaneous and unofficial vote of thanks, spoke with feeling of how much the genuine fellowship in prayer and action among the widely divergent members of the team had been due to Canon Warner's leadership. "Neither do I forget," he has written since, "his great help to me when my wife died, and how he took part in her funeral." Others have equally intimate reminiscences of his support in domestic troubles, for Hugh was on terms of personal friendship with all the leaders of Christian bodies in the town.

With the Roman Catholic priest, the late Canon Christall, he exchanged courtesies and annual Christmas cards. "I wish I had your church," Canon Christall remarked enviously; "I could fill it easily every Sunday!" And so he could, with Epsom full of foreign refugees and all the hospitals round staffed with Irish nurses. Nevertheless, as Hugh reminded him with a twinkle, "the church isn't exactly *un*filled, even now!" And on one occasion there was a rather surprising transfer of congregations when the bridal party arrived for a Roman Catholic wedding only to find that the priest, who was growing old and forgetful, had omitted to notify the registrar. In the general consternation the voice of an Anglican guest was heard. "I'm going to ring up the Vicar. *He* will know what to do!" The Vicar barely stopped to consider the situation. It was past noon. "Get into your car at once," he said to the bridegroom, "and drive straight to Westminster for a special licence." (Fortunately he was a surrogate.) "The office closes at 1 o'clock on a Saturday, but I will ring them up and tell them you are on the way. Tell the bride to stop crying and get on with her reception while you are gone, and I'll marry you in the parish church, according to the *Book of Common Prayer,* at 2.30." The wedding followed the reception, and the couple caught their train, their priest was relieved, the local press was delighted, and everyone was satisfied—except two members of the Vicar's own congregation, who protested staunchly against such truck with Rome—somewhat oddly, since the honours would seem to have rested with the Established Church. "Considering the pagan and semi-Christian couples one is expected to marry in Church," remarked Hugh, "it seems strange to be censured for marrying two Christians from another fold, when they are willing to conform!"

viii

If any couple married at St Martin's did not understand what they were doing when they undertook to "live together according to God's holy ordinance", it was no fault of Hugh's. His preparation for the sacrament of Marriage, as for that of Confirmation, was nothing if not thorough. Many confidences received from ill-adjusted or unhappy married couples made him determined to save others at the outset from unnecessary miseries and mistakes, whether physical, spiritual, or psychological; but he had learned a more discriminating technique since the early days, when he had been too ready to assume that every couple shared his own objective and uninhibited approach.

With the end of the war his main concern had shifted from Youth work to Marriage Guidance; a natural transition, for close experience of wartime youth, both in and out of the Services, had shown him the deep need, and the ready welcome, for Christian guidance on standards of behaviour and the relations of the sexes. Wartime marriages and separations had brought their own problems and demobilization was bringing more. All Hugh's energies were bent to the rebuilding of home life after the war years, to the welcoming of men and women returning from the Forces and absorbing them and their families into the life of the Church. At the same time he was, as ever, looking ahead, trying to lay the foundations of a more wholesome attitude to sex and a more stable conception of marriage for the next generation. Known already as a pioneer in this respect, he was a natural choice of the newly formed National Marriage Guidance Council in 1945 to be one of the Anglican representatives on their executive; and in 1946 he asked its founder, Dr Herbert Gray, to come to Epsom and address a special meeting with a view to establishing a local Council. Typically, the meeting took the form of a dinner party, to which he invited, to meet each other, all the social workers in the borough, both statutory and voluntary, who had hitherto been to one another but voices on a 'phone or addresses at an office. Typically, also, when a local Council had been established, he found it office quarters over a florist's near the market-place. "No one, man or woman," he said, "minds being seen ostensibly entering a flower-shop!"

For some time Hugh had given up travelling about the country to speak at Youth Rallies, under the increasing pressure and claims of parish life. But now he found himself even more widely in request at "Religion and Life" or "Home and Family" Weeks as a speaker on the Christian view of sex and marriage. In February 1948 the Dean of Guernsey invited him to the Channel Islands. Early that month he had slipped and fallen heavily on a snow-covered frozen road and injured his elbow. Making as little of it as possible, he came home and asked the monthly nurse (the sixth baby having recently arrived) to bind it up. She shook her head over it, but it was not until he had taken a funeral the following day, accompanying it to London for the cremation, and concealing acute pain throughout, that he eventually visited the local hospital for an X-ray. He was promptly ordered into King's College Hospital, where the elbow was suitably wired and encased in plaster. He insisted on discharging himself and travelling to Guernsey on the date arranged, with his arm still in plaster from the wrist up, to speak at their Home and Family Week. The Guernsey papers, reporting his speech, were the first to announce his appointment to an honorary Canonry in Guildford Cathedral.

It was a fatal habit of Hugh's to make too little of his own illnesses and to delay visits to the doctor far too long. He would take half a day in bed with a temperature, scotch it with large doses of aspirin, and then get up and go out on a cold winter's night to some meeting he felt he could not miss. Remonstrances were useless. "Man, you've a magnificent constitution," his doctor exclaimed, "but you *do* play tricks with it!" This was in striking contrast to his considerate care for others, especially children. When his own small son had to have an operation on his eyes, he would lie side by side with him blindfold on the nursery floor, rehearsing the experience beforehand, and imparting to a sensitive child a confidence and self-control that astonished the nurses of the children's ward. Hugh could spare any amount of time for things like that; none for "waiting about in surgeries" for himself.

In the summer of 1949, when investigating the roof of the church house to discover a leak, he slipped and caught his thumb-nail on a broken tile. Once again he delayed visiting the doctor until not only the thumb but other fingers had turned septic. Drastic antibiotic treatment spread over a period of months failed to prevent it infecting the other hand also. At last, in January 1950, having only two fingers left for use, and being unable to administer the Sacrament (he had with difficulty managed the Christmas services), he allowed a specialist to order him into hospital, where for six weeks he was treated for acute M and B poisoning.

It was an anxious time, the more so as five out of the six children were simultaneously ill with mumps. In the middle of it all one day Dr Gilbert Russell rang up, and, hearing that Hugh was in hospital, asked if a message might be taken to him. He himself was about to retire after a five years' term of office as Education Secretary to the Church of England Moral Welfare Council, in order to give his whole time to psychiatric practice. He had worked with Hugh for some time on the National Executive of the Marriage Guidance Council and there was nobody, he said, in the whole country that he would rather have to succeed him in Moral Welfare. The post would be advertised shortly in the *Church Times,* and he was anxious to know if Hugh would consider it, and if so to make sure that he applied. "Not," he pointed out, "that I can promise it to him. The appointment is the Council's, and they will have to consider all applications." "And there might, of course, be a far more suitable one?" "I can't imagine it," was the answer.

When he received the message Hugh was lying, as he lay all day, with his hands raw and skinless in a basin of solution which a nurse replenished at intervals with warm water. His whole body was covered with an intensely irritating rash and his face was disturbingly grey. He gazed straight in front of him, not speaking for a while; and then he said, "I think it's what I'm meant to do. And if I'm ever to do it at all it must be *now,* while I'm equal to it"—a comment which at the time sounded more ironic than ominous.

When he had recovered a little, and the hands were growing a new skin and could hold a pen, he wrote a long letter to his eldest son, explaining to him why he was proposing to make such a drastic move. It was like him to realize that what for him was the fulfilment of a life's vocation would be for the family a bewildering change; a smaller house and garden, a smaller income, a strange church, and father no longer the vicar but one of those who caught the train to Town each morning, except when he would be a sort of commercial traveller away for days at a time. Nevertheless, he pointed out, when at home in the evenings or at weekends, he would really *be* at home and able to have some private life, of which there is little in a vicarage. There might even be, also, some time to read.

ix

It was always a mystery when Hugh did his reading; probably during his many train journeys. He had a knack of skimming through a book, marking the paragraphs that struck him and extracting the essential arguments.

In 1947 the Haberdashers' Company had invited him to give the Golden Lectures, a series of lunch-hour addresses in a City church (the Savoy Chapel on this occasion) during Advent and Lent. For his Advent course he chose the title "Reaffirmation of Christian Morals", following it up in Lent 1948 (about the time of his visit to Guernsey) with "Modern Thought and Christian Belief". Moral philosophy and Christian ethics was an old line of country, but it was something of a feat, in the midst of the double pressure of parish life and marriage guidance work, to have kept up-to-date with the subjects of that second series : Scientific Humanism, Psychological Behaviourism, Biblical Criticism, Existentialism, Logical Positivism, and Marxism!

The double pressure had been steadily increasing for some time, and it was becoming clear, even before Gilbert Russell's message, that a choice would have to be made if justice was to be done to either. "Doing a hoosh" had never been a possibility in a parish the size of St Martin's, but now even the necessary visiting was beginning to suffer; though he did his best, by a system of wards and wardens (worked out by one of his curates after the wartime A.R.P. pattern), to ensure that news of newcomers, sick folk and those who most needed a visit did reach him and his staff.

His relations with his many curates had always been happy, and one of them had written from his first living, "I shall always remember what I owe to you. We learned from you what it means for a priest to give himself utterly to his people." But lately his colleagues had begun to have misgivings on that very point and to question whether any parish priest could combine a true cure of souls with engagements from John o' Groats to Land's End. They knew how many of his flock looked askance at the Vicar's marriage guidance work and resented his frequent absences from the parish. "Which will he choose, do you think?" asked Bishop Macmillan, calling one day at the vicarage when the Vicar was out, and sympathetically discussing the problem. "Parish work or Marriage Guidance?" Put like that it seemed an impossible choice. All his gifts and accumulated experience seemed to be calling him in one direction, and yet, as he had written to his father from Oxford, "One thing I do feel very certain; whatever I am called to do will be as an ordained man." It was the invitation to become Education Secretary of the Church's own Council for Sex, Marriage and the

Family (as he was fond of calling the Moral Welfare Council) that resolved his dilemma.

He explained his decision in two letters in the *Gazette*; one to prepare the way, the other when the news was out.

St Martin's Gazette, April 1950.

"Where would you put your finger if asked to point out the danger spot of Public life today, I wonder?

"Would you point to the political field . . . or to the international world . . . or to the tangled field of economics? Whichever you chose, you would have the same feeling : What can I possibly do about it?

"Closer at home, however, there is a still greater danger spot, and one which we can all do a good deal about. Every person born is first of all moulded by his home. The sort of politician, or statesman, or economist a man is likely to become will depend on the character which his mother, father and general early home training has given him.

"Yet home-life is threatened. The State is usurping more and more those duties of training which in other days fell to a child's parents. . . . In the years 1945, 1946 and 1947 the divorce rate doubled itself each year until 120,000 husbands and wives are involved each year. One in every four of first children start their lives outside marriage. The judges are confronted daily with the trial of hooligans who have 'coshed' someone over the head. Probation officers point out that they come from broken homes in nearly every case. The only remedy suggested as a rule for these toughs is either the 'cat' or more boys' clubs. What good can these clubs hope to be with boys whose homes have already ruined them?

"Surely it is the home that needs help before everything else. The over-riding duty of the Church is to help those who are getting married today and starting brand new homes."

St Martin's Gazette, May 1950.

"On my study desk, and in its cupboards, are nearly five hundred letters from all over England and Scotland from husbands and wives in distress. It is interesting, in these days of estrangement from the Church, that the writers should be looking to the Church for help in these matters. Among them are nearly one hundred from young men and women hoping soon to get married and who write to know where they can look for help in preparation for their wedding.

"In addition to this, you may know that within the last six months I have been asked by the Bishops concerned to travel to the dioceses of Oxford, Monmouth, Bangor, Norwich, Chelmsford, Guildford, Chichester and Manchester to lecture to clergy schools on 'Pastoral Preparation for Marriage'. I cannot deal with all this and run a parish properly as well.

"So many of you who are reading these words have locked up inside you the tragic knowledge of what failure to choose the right partner, or lack of similar ideals between you and your married partner, can mean to the atmosphere in which your children are spending their early years. You will see better than others the need for this sort of work. No purely social organization can give fully the help that is needed, for basically the need is spiritual; power to keep one's temper, to be considerate, to be willing to learn, to pray together about the problems of the home, to enter that environment of the spirit which we call public worship, to ride loosely to material ideals like comfort, ambition, big bank-balances, and social status, and to be able to suffer and at the same time to enrich the world by one's suffering.

"Then there are the psychological and physical adjustments, which go to the making of serene and contented homes. Here is for many the unrecognized cause of much unhappiness.

"There is a more subtle need, however, which, again, only the Church can meet. If public opinion is uncertain and pessimistic about marriage, then young people get infected with a low idea of what is possible, get easily disillusioned, miss the best and, too often, throw in the sponge altogether. How is public opinion to be changed? Only by out-thinking the philosophies of home and family life which contradict the Christian view. To do this in our day, it is necessary for the churchman to work in harness with the medical, psychological, and eugenic specialist. As a team, such people can publicize the scientific basis for the Christian understanding of marriage, commending it in such a way as to convince the non-churchman.

"This will entail research work, and will be part of the responsibility of the Church's Council for Marriage and Family Life of which I shall be Educational Secretary."

As when he left Bishopthorpe, his Diocesan deplored the move. Dr Montgomery Campbell had but newly come to the diocese and was now confronted with the necessity of appointing a new vicar to one of his largest cures. "Dear Warner," he wrote, "it is clear that you were born to vex me!"—a welcome gleam of humour amidst the gloom with which the news was received in the parish. Fearful lest parishioners should get wind of the appointment from the papers before hearing it from himself, Hugh called a special meeting of the P.C.C. in Holy Week. "You can tell the Vicar from me," blurted out a member of the Council, bursting into tears in the street, "that he has spoiled my Easter!" One of his choirmen called to ask if he could not reconsider the decision. Was he sure he was right to go when he was doing such good work in Epsom? Few could really understand the motives for the choice. Is it ever possible to understand a vocation? "Oh, well," said one, "I suppose you are right to better yourselves!" and on learning that *that* at least was not part of the picture looked more baffled than ever. But one lady did think that she had the clue. "I think you are very wise," she declared. "You see, it will be the stepping-stone to a bishopric!"

The appointment took effect from 1 July 1950, but Hugh did not resign the living until September, not wishing to upset the arrangements already made for staff holidays. It was the last big "overlap" to his story. As usual, he was full of plans, and already well into the next chapter of his life. But this time he found it less easy to disengage his heart. In the twelve years which covered the war years and the birth of half his family his roots had gone deep, as is shown by his last letters in the *Gazette*.

"My dear Friends,

"The sands of time are running out. As a rule I think a parish magazine should be addressed primarily to those who do not come to church. . . . In my last numbers I would rather address myself to you, that large number of regular worshippers who have shared with me so much that the outside world hasn't begun to understand."

"This is my 143rd letter I have written to you, and my last. . . . Wartime memories forge a link between us all that makes my leaving Epsom quite horrible, not only for me but also for my wife and family. To leave a parish like St Martin's is harder to bear than we thought possible. God bless you, children and grown-ups all, and especially those 1,425 babies Christened and 560 couples married in St Martin's since I first came among you."

Nevertheless, his final word is "look to the future, not backwards", and for the text of his farewell sermon he characteristically selected "Forgetting those things that are behind, and reaching forth to those things which are before, I press toward the mark for the prize of the high calling of God in Christ Jesus . . . but some WALK!"

The move took place at Michaelmas, to a house he had found in Dorking, and on Michaelmas Day 1950 we made our first Communion in Dorking Parish Church, also dedicated to St Martin, in the beautiful lady chapel which is thronged with angels and crowned with a mosaic of the Risen and Ascended Christ seated in glory. 'I am He that liveth and was dead," runs the text; and the angels bear a scroll, "I look for the Resurrection of the Dead, and the life of the world to come." "I think this will be a nice church for the family to worship in," said Hugh.

8

COURSE FINISHED

Moral Welfare

Now, through the land, his cure of souls he stretched;
And like a primitive apostle preached,
Still cheerful; ever constant to his call;
By many followed, loved by most, admired by all.
John Dryden : Character of a Good Parson

i

PENCILLED in Hugh's tiny writing on the last page of one of his engagement diaries during the war are these lines :

> For these 5 breathless years we had to run
> To keep abreast of Time's increasing pace :
> Could we have had some respite from that race
> We should regret now fewer things undone.

The war years with their strain and loss of sleep took their toll, but the lines seem even more applicable to the increasing pace of Hugh Warner's five breathless years of Moral Welfare work. What he packed into these years of travelling, lecturing, writing, committee work, and sheer personal self-giving seems incredible, especially when one knows that after his serious illness in Epsom he was never the same man again. Five years later, during his final illness, a house surgeon at the hospital protested at this statement. "Why, it's in the last five years that he has made his reputation!" "If I am to do it at all, it must be done now," Hugh had said then. But he was not thinking of making a reputation.

"This pupil is probably the most consistent boy in the school." So his schoolmaster had written, and so, as his story has shown, he had ever been. The intensive work of these last years was but the fulfilment of something foreshadowed long ago in the letters to his mother from Oxford and to his fiancée from Westcott House, and all his "many parts" merged into the final rôle of Education Secretary to the Church of England Moral Welfare Council. No one could have been more fitted to expand the educational part of moral welfare, for education had always figured prominently both in his youth work and in his parish programmes; and in the marriage guidance work that he had done so far he had been especially concerned with the educational development through lectures to engaged couples, youth clubs, and sixth forms. In his Birmingham days, when as S.C.M. secretary he tried to solve the courting and matrimonial problems of the students who gave him their confidence, his psychological studies had first made clear to him how many of these sad tangles were due to ignorance—sheer ignorance, he had once written, "of how men and women work".

The advocates of sex education in schools, he felt, had reversed rather than solved the problem. The older generation had often been brought up in disastrous ignorance of their own mechanism, but their Victorian parents and chaperones had taught them a strict highway code. The modern idea was to teach them "the works" and launch them on the highway of life without any guidance in handling such high-powered mechanism with safety to themselves and consideration for others. It was the Church's duty, in Hugh's view, to see that both physiological and theological ignorance were dispelled together, and that the true training in sex involved both the understanding of what it is and the appreciation of God's purpose in Creation. Old-fashioned obscurantism and the purely biological approach could have equally unfortunate results.

As an example of the obscurantist attitude, he could well remember, in his own schooldays, being given a book which purported to tell a boy "all he ought to know", but unfortunately all the really enlightening and interesting pages had been carefully cut out, leaving him with a baffled sense of unnecessary mystery. He looked back on the episode with amusement, admitting with his customary justice that the donor meant well and was probably courageous and enlightened for those times in broaching the subject at all. But he was reminded of this early experience again in 1926 at one of the Student Conferences in America, when he had been called upon to advertise the Conference Bookstall. Fresh from Swanwick where he had taken the chair for a meeting by Dr Herbert Gray, whose robust Christian approach to sex relationships had deeply impressed him, he enthusiastically recommended Gray's *Men, Women and God,* the pioneer book on the subject, drawing attention especially to the useful appendix on "Some of the Physical Facts". After the conference an aggrieved knot of students confronted him beside the bookstall. "We bought the book you recommended," they said, "but where is this appendix you talked about?" Hugh investigated. The Puritan U.S.A. had censored the appendix.

It was with memories like these to guide him, together with a good deal of experience since both of young people's questions and of marital misunderstandings, that in 1946-7 Hugh embarked on the making of his film strip, *Men and Women: The Christian View of Human Life.* He had been on the Executive Committee of the National Marriage Guidance Council since its inception, and the possibility of film strips had been canvassed there for some time. But, as

Dr Gilbert Russell wrote of him in the *Marriage Guidance Bulletin* after his death, "While others were still debating what might be done, if only it were possible to find out where to begin, Hugh Warner had probably begun: he had worked out a plan or sketched a syllabus or drafted a memorandum: the thing was already under way. . . . If film strips had been found effective in some field of education, he was not content to 'consider whether perhaps there might not, in time, be some place for them, under suitable conditions, and in appropriate hands. . . .' He would make one and see." It is the "Now" and "At once" of the Central Youth Council story over again.

He tried the film strip lectures out on his Confirmation classes in Epsom, being careful to give a showing first of all to the candidates' parents. The word went round; teachers, social workers, parents' associations and young mothers' groups asked for a showing, and gradually it became known among all who were interested in the subject of sex education, outside as well as inside the parish.

The headmasters of two public schools in the vicinity, Epsom College and St John's, Leatherhead, asked him to give two lectures annually to the boys, one at the beginning of the school year to new boys and one at the end to "leavers". Each of these was followed up a week later by a question session, the questions having been written down and sent in anonymously after the lecture. The perusal of those questions should have dispelled the doubts and suspicions of any old-fashioned objectors to sex education as "putting ideas into children's heads". The headmistress of a girls' school, too, was astonished to see some of the questions sent in by her younger girls. "Please, what is a test-tube baby?" is sufficiently disconcerting from an eleven-year-old. Children whose parents take the more sensational papers cannot be brought up in a Victorian vacuum; and Hugh, whose own sense of wonder and awe at creation grew with knowledge, never confused mystery with mystification or innocence with ignorance. His own standpoint, and that which he aimed to communicate, was that of the 139th Psalm, which the Moral Welfare Council so appositely chose for his Memorial Service:

> Thou hast fashioned me behind and before, and
>   laid thine hand upon me . . .
> I will give thanks unto thee, for I am fearfully
>   and wonderfully made: marvellous are thy
>   works, and that my soul knoweth right well.

That religious background was all-important. From his youth work he knew that, while the twelve-year-old is objectively curious about the scientific facts, a purely biological approach is no help to the adolescent, whose chief interest (as the written questions clearly showed) is in behaviour problems. ("Is petting wrong? And why? And how far may one go?") Hugh was always at his best in handling tricky personal questions, and it was after one of these sessions that the Headmaster of St John's exclaimed, "The Church doesn't know its job! If I were Archbishop I wouldn't let you be wasted on a parish. You should be seconded to do this in every boys' school in the country!"

Hugh was doing his best by the dissemination, on request, of the film strip and the accompanying script. But that, as many remarked, was not quite the same thing. The most important factor in the effect of the lecture was the personality of the lecturer. What could in less sure hands cause embarrassment was completely devoid of offence when delivered with that clear, level, objective voice, that disarming frankness and instinctive tact, and when the most awkward questions were met with composure, sympathy and humour. There were those who were inclined to think that he made it all seem a little *too* easy. Sex, after all, has been the major problem of mankind throughout the centuries. But to Hugh's mind brooding over difficulties was no way to overcome them. Nothing annoyed him more than to have his pitch queered by an embarrassed chairman who would introduce him as having "come to speak to us to-night on a very difficult subject". ("Ridiculous fellow, to go and make them all self-conscious at the outset!") Embarrassment and self-consciousness betoken fear, and the way to deal with fear, of sex as of other high explosives, was to face it, accept it, analyse it and so learn how to deal with it. "Remember you are a Christian, not a jelly fish!"

ii

It was not surprising that, having watched his early film strip experiments and worked with him on the Marriage Guidance Council, Gilbert Russell should have picked Hugh Warner as the man to carry further the educational work of moral welfare. But, as he had warned him, it was the Council's appointment; and when the post was advertised there were other applicants not without their qualifications. Miss Ena Steel, the General Secretary, has described Hugh's interview. "It was really funny. It was quite difficult to make him understand that he was only 'short-listed'. I don't think he really grasped it at all. In his mind he was already Education Secretary. Oh no, it wasn't arrogance. Never that with Hugh. It was his extraordinary single-mindedness. Once he got on to a track he just went straight ahead, always. There were no 'ifs' or 'buts'." How were the Council to know that this was what he had to do, and that it had to be now? Only afterwards, looking back, did somebody write, "God raises up the right man at the right time to do the right work."

The appointment made, Hugh's first sensation was one of release. After the distracting tension of the last few years he was free to concentrate on one issue, and give his whole mind to the task. It was not, of course, his first contact with moral welfare. During his incumbency of St Martin's he had helped to form the Epsom and Leatherhead Association and co-operated very closely with the moral welfare worker. She had always looked on him as the one in whose discretion she could confide and who really understood her problems; while he regarded, and taught the parish to regard, her work as no "extra", but as an essential part of the seeking and saving ministry of the Church. It was another of his unpopular causes. "I can't think where all these people come from," declared an aristocratic lady in disgust. "I'm sure there weren't so many in the last vicar's time"—a remark which would have tickled Hugh's sense of humour had he not felt angry that it should have been made in the hearing of a sensitive "illegitimate" mother.

"May I ask you," he had written in the *Epsom Gazette,* before the yearly collection for the People's Offering for Moral Welfare, "to challenge the apathy of so many towards the moral welfare work of this and neighbouring parishes. You are sure to meet people who say, 'Why do anything for the unmarried mother?' . . . Tell them it is the *babies* who suffer. If a girl is merely ostracized by everybody, including her own parents, how is she to offer that security to her child which is the birthright of every baby? . . . Here locally our own moral welfare worker has had within a matter of days to deal with the mother of a baby abandoned in a railway carriage, and four children whose mother ran away, leaving a bedridden husband to cope with them, the youngest about six months. She has at any time between sixty and seventy women to watch over, and such self-sacrificing work in the name of the Church deserves surely something better than a blank refusal to help. The other day she found one poor little mite of four sitting all hunched up in an armchair, clasping and unclasping her little hands for hours on end, and refusing to speak because her father whom she loved had told the family he had fallen in love with another woman and was leaving them. Unless something is done that small girl will lose her reason. The father has now gone away, and the mother is desperate."

It was not only with educational experiments, but with much practical experience of case-work of this kind, that Hugh Warner came armed to the central Moral Welfare Council.

iii

Yet another arrow in the new Secretary's quiver was his flair for journalism. His first contact with headquarters had been in June 1948, when the Literature Committee decided to revise a publication of the White Cross League (now fused with the Moral Welfare Council), called *The Threshold of Marriage*. Dr Russell had suggested that the Vicar of Epsom, at that time specializing in marriage guidance work, should be co-opted on to the Committee. They wanted to incorporate into the text adequately, but not disproportionately, the physical information which had hitherto been treated as a thing apart in a separate pamphlet obtainable on request. They were also concerned about the serious problem of so many newly-weds living with in-laws; and in general they considered the subject-matter, excellent as it was, needed bringing up to date. But it was the style that called forth Hugh's criticism. No couple nowadays, he maintained, would read a book right through that looked so dull and unattractive, with long sentences, no headlines or sub-titles, and paragraphs that sometimes took up the whole of a page. He was asked if he would draft a new format. Needless to say, it was as good as done.

When it was published in 1949 it immediately became "news", both on the B.B.C. and in the Press. The Church of England had written a book about Marriage. This amused those who knew it had been widely used since 1932 and already had a circulation of 24,000, but it showed that modern technique had put it on the map. Dr Russell, being asked by the News Editor of the *Daily Express* for further information, referred him to "the man who had done the job". It was late in the evening when Hugh took the 'phone call, but with his usual promptness he immediately despatched, as requested, an article and a photograph—the first that came to hand, off the drawing-room piano, taken of him in his Luton days. Next day the *Express* demanded a series of articles on Modern Marriage, and sent down a photographer to take a contemporary likeness. Readers of that journal noted with surprise that the new contributor appeared to have aged twenty years overnight.

So began Canon Warner's connection with the Press, which resulted in his becoming, as a railway porter recognizing him from his photographs once told him, "the best-known clergyman in the Church of England".

Not all the Vicar's flock were pleased at his excursions into journalism, and an indignant relation, when an article appeared in one of the least savoury Sunday papers, wrote demanding, "Why on earth do you let Hugh write for such a *lousy* paper?" "That's exactly why," was Hugh's reply;

an echo of the classic answer to such protests, "They that are whole have no need of a physician. . . ."

Like the schoolboys' questions, the pile of correspondence that now appeared daily on the breakfast table should have given the critics something to ponder. To the Press itself Sex and Religion might be simply good copy or a safe stunt, but not to the hundreds who wrote in genuine trouble or bewilderment to a man who seemed able to speak to their condition and untangle their problems. This correspondence was an added burden to the last few years at Epsom, for Hugh took it very seriously and answered many individually, often more than once. When one in real difficulty gave neither surname nor address, and the Editor would not print his answer in his weekly column as "not of sufficient general interest", he was really troubled. He was sensitive to all requests for help, and distressed that any should ask for it in vain.

It was characteristic that having once again found himself an "expert" *malgré lui,* he set to work to equip himself more fully for the part. He took the full course of training for a marriage guidance counsellor, and to the books on ethics and psychology already on his shelves there were now added the latest or the authoritative works on Moral Theology, Sociology, Sexology, Education and the like. His old interest in medicine revived also. His marriage guidance work brought him many contacts with the medical profession, and a friend passed on to him the current numbers of the *British Medical Journal*. In days when few people knew very much about the Rhesus factor he would quietly lend a relevant book or article on the subject to a busy G.P. before sending a couple for medical consultation. "A (Christian) leader must be right abreast of the advance guard of knowledge in all its branches," he had written as a young man at the University, "and able to compete with the best non-Christian intellects." But he was equally aware of the workings of the non-intellectual mind, and could filter down the conclusions of scholars and experts to the "man in the pub".

This, so said Joe Brayshaw, the General Secretary of the National Marriage Guidance Council, was Hugh's supreme gift and his rare value. He could "talk with kings" (or at any rate with Archbishops!) "nor lose the common touch". Few men can, when occasion demands, draft a report or write a paper which commands respect, such as his address on Contraception to the Oecumenical Institute at Bossey, printed in *Theology* in January 1954[1] and at the same time turn out articles which will be accepted by popular dailies and read with approval in the NAAFI. The secret was that his writing grew directly out of his experience. In the ecclesiastical, as in the educational or agricultural sphere, it is sometimes a grievance that "those who can, do; those who can't, plan". Hugh's plans (and he loved plans!) grew out of his doings, and the success of his work for marriage guidance and for moral welfare was the fruit and the measure of his success as a parish priest and as a family man.

Nowhere, perhaps, was this so clearly seen as in the series of booklets on Sex Education which were produced in his first year as Education Secretary. He had already divided his film strip into two parts, a senior and a junior; now he set to work to write a graded series of small books which would be suitable for different ages. In both cases he took enormous trouble over scientific accuracy, consulting specialists and inviting criticism. But his inimitable method of imparting information was due to his own intimate knowledge of each age-group. The reception of the series was instructive. Each

[1] Based on an unpublished manuscript written by the Reverend Dr Sherwin Bailey.

group approved the number intended for it and thought little of the others. The Mothers' Union particularly liked *Puzzled Parents* (for parents of young children) and *Where Did I Come From?* (for the eight-year-olds), but was more doubtful about *The Christian View of Sex,* with its objective discussion of contraception. *The Times Educational Supplement,* on the other hand, considered this "far the most valuable of the series", but was slightly superior about the junior grades, surmising that the author, perhaps, had not had much experience of children! The mother of two boys, a young one and a teenager, wrote that it was amusing to hear the younger one insisting on the older one reading *his* book, and the older one maintaining that his own was far the better. As Hugh Warner's own family at the time ranged in age from twenty to four years old, it was not surprising that he had hit the target every time. Some years later a priest who sent a contribution to the Hugh Warner Memorial Fund wrote to the Council :

"I fear the amount is quite unrepresentative of the gratitude I feel to Hugh Warner for all he did (and is still doing) in the sphere of happy marriages. What wouldn't I have given for his booklets forty years ago—and even at my relatively advanced age I have derived considerable help from his writings. I find them invaluable in my dealings with those about to marry, with young married people, with parents and with adolescents, in my own parish and in a much wider sphere. He has indeed deserved well of the Church and of the community."

Throughout his time as Education Secretary Hugh continued to write, at intervals, for the Press. He became the recognized spokesman on questions of sex, marriage or morals that cropped up from time to time, and he could always be counted upon for a prompt answer to any challenge. On holiday in Cornwall one summer he was asked for an article "by return" on a current controversial topic. He did not wait to write or post it, but went straight to the nearest telephone kiosk and dictated it at length while impatient queues formed outside. He would never let the Church's case go by default, and many a time took the train to Town at the week-end in order to hand in his letter, answering some attack on Christian standards, before the paper "went to bed", rather than miss a post and the psychological moment. "I hope 'Moral Welfare' is going to answer that," said someone apropos a letter in an evening paper after he had gone. "It will be answered," replied Miss Steel, "but not as quickly as when we had Hugh Warner at the office."

There are occasions when a man is betrayed by his best qualities. In 1951 a popular illustrated weekly announced that it was going to feature a series of frank discussions on sex and marriage between medical and scientific experts, giving due consideration to moral values. Hugh, rather too precipitately this time, officially welcomed the venture and, in effect, bade it Godspeed. But after a few issues it was clear that something had gone very wrong, and many parents, teachers, and others responsible for the young were growing more and more unhappy over the tone and influence of the articles. Hugh had to write again expressing disappointment that the "moral values" had never even been considered, and that things had been said which no spokesman for the Church could condone. The Editor asked if he would join the panel and contribute to the discussion so that the Church's point of view might be expressed. Hugh consented, on condition that he was allowed his full say and was reported without "editing". The condition was granted, but it was too late. The damage had been done and schools and families had cancelled their orders for the paper, so that many who had seen the unfortunate articles never read the Church's criticism. It is permissible to hope, however, that it was read in those quarters where sales had correspondingly increased. If so, the Christian position had not quite gone by default.

iv

"Do you know a man called Canon Warner?" one of his sons disingenuously asked a journalist acquaintance, not revealing the relationship. "Canon Warner? Oh yes, the Keep the Party Clean man. Quite a good chap!" was the answer.

Hugh enjoyed and valued his connection with the Press, but he fearlessly attacked its less desirable features, and during his last years sought to mobilize Christian opinion against the salacity and near-pornography of some Sunday and other papers. Many years before, in Bishopthorpe, he had been specially concerned with the effect on young people of the indiscriminate advertisement and sale of contraceptives and accompanying pornographic literature in the back-street shops and even the market-place of York, and had addressed the Ruri-Decanal Conference on the subject of obscene literature. Now in 1954 his publication, *Threatened Standards,* gave chapter and verse for the indictment. But it did not include, for he had no desire to publish or advertise, the gallery of illustrations he had collected from papers and magazines of all kinds, and which he displayed to an *ad hoc* committee drawn from various Church, Youth, and other societies to discuss the problem, brought to a head by the type of publicity given in the Press to the Kinsey Report.

Hugh had always responded instinctively to the delighted wonder of great artists and sculptors at the beauty of the human form, and it saddened him that young people should have this innocent approach spoiled for them by the prostitution of semi-nudity in "cheap" and suggestive magazines. He tried to anticipate and counteract this influence, in his books for teen-agers, by making use of good art to help to form a true and wholesome outlook. His campaigns were always positive, not prudish. Many envied his antiseptic innocence, but could not emulate it; and the brunt of the work was left to him. When he asked some of the committee to share the burden of watching and "vetting" the worst of the publications, one confessed, "We just don't like doing it. It leaves such a nasty taste in the mouth; it makes one feel guilty, having read the thing at all." "Have I got to read this book?" asked a judge, trying the case of an exceptionally evil publication which Hugh had brought to the notice of the Home Secretary; "it makes me feel physically sick." "I *was* sick," Hugh admitted at home. "I just couldn't show it to anyone at the office, or anywhere." Yet the author had the effrontery to write to him personally, from abroad, asking if he would be good enough to explain the British law on the subject, so that he might know just how near the wind it was safe to sail in future. Such is the shamelessness of evil, and there was little Hugh did not know about it before he had finished. But though it might make him sick at heart, and in literal fact, it left no scar on his soul. Those who realized what had gone to the producing of *Threatened Standards* agreed that they knew nobody but Hugh Warner who could have undertaken the task and come through so completely unsullied. "Purity of heart is not a phrase I use easily," one wrote, "but it is the essential quality of Hugh."

Pure in heart he was, but neither puritan nor purist. He

was never one to denigrate romance in the interests of Christian morality, though he might have a good deal to say about its specious substitute, glamour. The real condemnation of the glamour cult in his eyes was not that it is romantic, but precisely that it is not; that it is such a sad, sordid, sentimental travesty of the glory of Christian love. "What a lot they miss!" was his invariable comment on the exponents of "modern" sub-Christian views of love and marriage; and in his dealings with those whose love affairs or marriages had come to grief he was more saddened by the tarnishing of an ideal than shocked by the transgressing of a code. This is clearly seen in his classic pamphlet *On Falling in Love*, and again in his last and most charming contribution to the Press, an article in a woman's magazine, *Love Without Tears*. "If only we could show people this, stripped of false tinsel, and against the background of God and Home!" as he had written in his youth. That was still the spirit in which he waged his tireless crusade against the forces in society that conspire to blur the ideal and make it for many so difficult of attainment.

v

Since Hugh Warner had been in Epsom the initiator and the moving spirit of both Marriage Guidance Council and Moral Welfare Association, he had been less conscious of the distinction between the two than of the possibility of working in harmony. After his first lecture as Education Secretary to a group of students, Miss Kennedy, the Deputy General Secretary, took him to task. These were potential church workers, she pointed out, and needed more specific briefing on their particular task of co-operating with the clergy rather than a general recommendation to Marriage Guidance Councils. "Show me where I was wrong," said

Hugh, "and give me another session with them. I'll put it right." He was the least touchy man alive in respect of criticism, and he set to work once more to master his subject.

His first real interest in moral welfare dated from the time when he had heard Miss Higson, the pioneer in its educational work, lecture to the ordinands in Westcott House. Now he found himself one of the team on whom her mantle had fallen, and of all his work as Education Secretary he looked upon his visits to the theological colleges as the most valuable. His days of willing acceptance of any and every invitation to speak to small sporadic groups were over. He knew he must concentrate now on training leaders, through social workers' conferences, teachers' training colleges, clergy schools, and the like; but the key people, he felt, were the ordinands. Of the twenty-eight theological colleges in England and Wales, of every type of churchmanship, he was a regular and welcome visitor at all but two. He was prepared to be all things to all men if by any chance he might help some. And what he could give them, staying as he often did for two or three days at a time in the college, was much more than can be communicated through the most thorough course of lectures. If a priest is to be able to help confirmation candidates, adolescents in difficulty, couples coming to put up the banns, families in domestic trouble, the unhappily married or the unhappily *un*married (too often overlooked), the inverts and the perplexed, and all the penitents with problems, it is essential that he should himself be free from emotional knots and tangles. Perhaps Hugh Warner's greatest service to the Church, though like the seed growing secretly it cannot easily be estimated, may prove to have been done in those private interviews with young men, married and unmarried, in training for the Ministry, so many of whom brought him their own difficulties after the lectures

were over that often he was kept up till late into the night,
Some of them, like the correspondent quoted earlier, found
in his rare combination of Christianity and psychology a
refreshingly new and hopeful approach to some problem or
temptation in respect of which they were growing weary of
conventional penances and exhortations. And perhaps they
learned from him part of the secret of his own success in
dealing with persons; his gentleness, humility, and rare gift
of listening.

Clergymen in the parishes, too, were grateful for his help;
for in their time as ordinands there had been no training in
the preparation for marriage which the Church (and also the
recent Denning Report) recognized to be the most constructive answer to divorce. "He gave something to parish
priests", was the verdict of one diocese, "that no one else
seems quite able to give, and he left them not only enlightened but greatly heartened. Nothing in the difficult work of
dealing with baffling personal relationships in the parish ever
seemed quite so hard again after they had listened to Hugh
Warner!" To similar comments from both English Pro-
vinces, as also from the Church in Wales, might be added
the tribute of one who had heard him lecture at St Augus-
tine's College, Canterbury: "We in New Zealand realize
what we owe to him."

For the Chaplains' Department of the R.A.F., he conducted Quiet Days and courses of lectures; and on one occasion he was invited to lecture to American troops stationed
in England; an opening he would have wished to follow up,
had he lived.

In April 1953 all this educational work was given fresh
impetus when Hugh launched a campaign for Education for
Marriage and Family Life in an address to the British
Council of Churches in Birmingham. It is typical that, hav-

ing launched it through the Council of Churches, he immediately took practical steps to put it into effect in his own
Communion. He worked out detailed suggestions for the
Anglican Church, which were sent out through the Moral
Welfare Council to all Diocesan Bishops, and several dioceses
are still implementing or adapting these suggestions. Moreover, as Chairman of the Sub-Committee of the British
Council of Churches for Sex, Marriage and the Family, he
tried to help his Nonconformist friends also to work out the
campaign in their own way.

vi

In 1951 Mrs Eirene White's Bill, proposing automatic
divorce after seven years' separation, came before the House
of Commons, and Canon Warner helped to brief the opposition to it. Opinion was obviously strong and so divided that
the Government promised a Royal Commission on the whole
subject of Marriage and Divorce, and for the next three years
there was unceasing work at the office collecting and collat-
ing material for the Church's evidence. As Education Secretary, Hugh drafted a questionnaire for study circles to be
circulated in the dioceses. As usual he was so anxious to
"take the current when it serves" that he was a little too
precipitate for the Council. Some felt that with more re-
vision, and perhaps another hand upon it, it might have
been improved and have produced more valuable results.
Even so, there was value in the scheme by which numerous
discussion groups were so quickly formed throughout the
country, bringing clergy, doctors, lawyers, social workers
and others together to clarify the issues and pool their conclusions.

On 28 May 1952 Canon Warner and Dr Gilbert Russell

accompanied the Archbishop of Canterbury and the Bishop of London to present the Church's evidence before the Royal Commission. The point that Canon Warner himself stressed at some length, and produced impressive statistics to prove, was that if, as was frequently claimed, the main object of increasing divorce facilities was to regularize and reduce the number of unsatisfactory separations and illicit unions, it had been singularly unsuccessful in achieving this object. Every time divorce was made easier, not only did the number of divorces increase (which might be expected), but the number of separations not only did not decrease but increased in proportion; a fact which confirmed the Church's contention that divorce is more of a disease than a remedy and constitutes in itself a growing threat to the stability of marriage as an institution. He would have gone on to elaborate this at some length, but the Archbishop's time was limited and the Commission wished to hear more of his evidence. But after the session a member of the Commission came up to speak to Hugh. "I'm sorry we had to cut you short," he said, "but I was most interested in your statistics, and should like to hear some more about them. I think they are very important."

At the same time someone else was waiting to waylay him. "It just proves", His Grace had commented on those same statistics, "that *facilis descensus Averno*." "Always supposing", countered Lord Moreton of Henryton, with the impartial caution of the perfect chairman, "that we are agreed that it *is* Avernus!" The unfortunate stenographer looked helplessly round the exalted gathering for someone who appeared approachable as well as knowledgeable, and caught the eye of the clergyman with the cheerful and friendly smile. "Would you mind", she asked him afterwards, "explaining to me that Latin joke of the Archbishop's? Something about Avernus?" It was equally important to Hugh that a worried typist should claim his attention as that an eminent lawyer should demand his statistics.

In *The Church and Marriage*, being the evidence presented to the Commission, there is a summary of extracts from the evidence, compiled by Canon Warner, to show what would be the effects of easy divorce. Put plainly and cogently, the argument is that easy divorce will (1) distort ideals, (2) foster lawlessness, (3) encourage self-will, (4) weaken the sense of obligation, (5) offer a cloak of respectability to sin, (6) encourage extra-marital affairs, (7) encourage evasion of parenthood, (8) contribute to family instability, and (9) offer children a precedent for divorce.

In all his speaking and writing on the subject it was this long-term view of the effect on society in general that he kept steadily to the fore, in contrast to the constant special pleading on behalf of hard cases. Several times he crossed swords with the most persistent advocate of marriage "reform", Sir Alan Herbert, and was planning, in the last months before his illness, to challenge him to a public debate on the same platform. The Hugh Warner who was ready to discuss with a Buddhist priest in his S.C.M. days, or a Professor Joad in his diaconate, was quite equal to taking on A. P. H., and was only too eager to "pin him down". Sparring in the Press was too elusive, especially when an editor seemed to think that fair-play was satisfied by giving Sir Alan space for a full article on a centre page with headlines and photograph, and first ignoring the reply of the Church's spokesman, and then, pricked by a strong protest from Lambeth, printing it, greatly condensed, in the unimportant form of a letter to the editor. Hugh, however, sent his complete article to Sir Alan, and they exchanged some correspondence on the matter, the upshot of which was that in his book,

The Right to Marry, Sir Alan referred to Canon Warner as "a very fair and friendly controversialist". Counting on this friendliness and fairness, before the publication of *The Right to Marry* the author somewhat disingenuously wrote to his opponent asking if he would be good enough to set down for him just what the Church's position was, as he would like to be sure he had understood it properly. Hugh might be guileless, but he was not so naïve as to concur, and he replied courteously that he too was thinking of writing a book, and he hoped it would make the Church's position perfectly plain.

Divorce and Remarriage: What the Church Believes and Why was Hugh Warner's reply to *The Right to Marry*. It was published in November 1954. Hugh was by then in hospital, seriously ill, but he asked that a complimentary copy should be sent from the office to his "sparring partner". The book shows signs of haste for, consciously or unconsciously, Hugh was writing against time; but his capacity for writing on two separate planes was never better illustrated than in the two Appendices, a remarkable "right and left" in the shape of an article intended for *Punch* and a sermon preached on Quinquagesima Sunday, 24 February 1954, in Westminster Abbey. *Punch* had rejected the article, but only after keeping it many weeks unable to decide whether to print it or not. It was, perhaps, too bold of Hugh to have invaded A. P. H.'s own preserve! But it is the Quinquagesima sermon that shows him at his most convinced and most convincing, and reveals too the deep sympathy and feeling for persons which was always there beneath all the arguments.

Non-Anglican colleagues on the Marriage Guidance Council were sometimes puzzled, knowing Hugh's personality, at what seemed to them surprising rigidity on this one subject. They did not see that his opposition to divorce was the necessary counterpart of his passionate belief in Christian marriage. He was no doctrinaire sociologist, but his whole experience, in youth work, in parish life, and as a marriage guidance counsellor, had proved to him increasingly that the greatest obstacle to educational work among the young, or to reconciliation in threatened marriages, was the mental climate of an overwhelmingly divorce-minded society. "Opportunity makes the thief", and the possibility of divorce is in itself a suggestion and temptation to the irresponsible. He knew how often girls "in trouble" sat in the moral welfare worker's office saying, "Everything will be all right. He's going to persuade his wife to divorce him and then he'll marry me." "All right for whom?" Hugh would ask. For the reluctant wife and the lawful family discarded, under pressure, for a new infatuation? He remembered the small child clasping and unclasping her hands for hours on end, and the mother who was desperate. "We meet our hard cases too," he wrote, "but they need a more bracing sympathy." That he was wonderfully able to give. After one of his lectures a woman in the audience rose to ask how he would advise a friend of hers whose genuinely hard case she described. Why should she have to renounce the chance of personal happiness? With great gentleness and understanding Hugh replied, "I do not think we should underrate the pain and sacrifice involved. But could she not look upon it as her share of the Cross of Christ, and offer it to Him to use it for the redemption of the sins of our society? Every such act of heroism makes it easier for others to make a stand, and only by such witness shall we re-establish Christian standards." The look on the questioner's face as she sat down revealed that she suddenly saw the situation from an entirely new angle.

Hugh's sympathy was with those hard cases that divorce does not relieve but create; the unwilling partner to a divorce who, as he once put it, "has far more truly 'lost her husband' than a widow, but won't have the sympathy a widow has". "I can never forget," wrote one such wife, "how he helped me at the time my divorce went through. But my deepest gratitude is for the way he led me back to Christianity. I can't really explain it in words, but it was as if everything fell into place." She was not the only one to experience this positive quality of Hugh's marriage guidance. If the marriage could not be mended, the life might be. Underneath the marriage counsellor Hugh was always the priest whose concern is not with cases but with souls.

For this reason he could never adopt the ultra-rigorist position of those who would permanently excommunicate all re-married divorcés. The distinction in his mind between sin and sinner was very clear here. It is one thing to maintain that a course of action is wrong, and to refuse categorically to condone it, by the use, for instance, of the Church's marriage service; quite another to brand all who take that course as "notorious and open evil-livers". Many might take a wrong course in good faith and with no uneasy conscience. In a society that has generally been able to regard "lawful" and "right" as synonymous, those who are set on bending the law to make divorce ever more easy, common and socially respectable have been responsible for much darkening of counsel. Theirs, therefore, is the greater sin. This is the point at which the Church should be adamant; not in pastoral dealings with individuals.

As for the contention that the "re-married" should prove repentance by cessation of intercourse, that seemed an invention of Mr Legality's mind, an indication that divorce was being regarded as a purely technical offence rather than, as

it always appeared to Hugh, a sin against the law of Love.
One does not atone for betraying one pledge by dishonour-
ing another. Once a new home and family has been established (however wrongly), it carries with it its own obliga-
tions. No one, for instance, demands that an unmarried
mother should prove her repentance by ceasing to foster
and cherish her child. As so often in life, Hugh would point
out, the worst result of taking a wrong turning is that at the
next cross-roads you cannot take an absolutely "right" one,
but only choose between two doubtful ones. One's duty then
is to decide which is the least wrong, and in those circumstances that will be the *right* course, and will often consist in
literally making the best (even the very best) of a bad job.

He once tried to make this general position plain in a
speech at a Diocesan conference, and was severely criticized
for preaching the pernicious doctrine of a "relative" instead
of an "absolute" morality. "But they are looking for an
absolute in the wrong place," he protested afterwards, "in
an abstract moral code, whereas we have to be moral in given
concrete situations and relations. That is why Love is the
fulfilling of the Law. But we have a double duty always; to
discover what is right in our particular circumstances, *and
then to do it*. The first is bound to be relative; the second is
absolute." When individuals brought him their many problems, asking "What am I to do?" he would try to make
them face the question honestly. "What is the right thing for
me to do, *now*, in *these* circumstances?"—circumstances of
which he always showed such a sympathetic grasp and
understanding.

vii

This concern for people, what Archbishop Fisher has described as "his genius for friendship and true shepherding",

he carried over from his work as a parish priest into his new work on its nation-wide scale. Individuals with problems, from all over the country and of all nationalities, not only called to see him at Church House but were waiting in his study at home when he returned from a day's work at the office or a week away lecturing. Dorking had no local marriage guidance panel, and the Citizens' Advice Bureau, remembering with relief that Canon Warner's house was just up the road, directed inquirers with matrimonial problems to that address. And still the letters came from all quarters, demanding advice and comfort. On hearing of his final illness a neighbour exclaimed, "I'm not surprised. Canon Warner has been bearing *everybody's* burdens."

Such confidences are a heavy strain for they cannot be shared, even with one's nearest and dearest. No one believed more truly than Hugh that there should be no secrets between husband and wife, but that did not include betraying other people's secrets. Sometimes this had led to awkward situations in Epsom, when someone, finding the vicar out but the vicar's wife at home, would say, "Never mind. You'll do as well, I dare say. I expect he has told you all about my trouble, hasn't he?" To say "Certainly not!" might sound a little unsympathetic; and one had to ask non-committally "how things were going", and hope the visitor would drop a clue. One man sat through a long afternoon, gazing blankly at the fire and refusing all offers of cups of tea, simply saying at intervals, "Canon Warner told me what would happen and I wouldn't listen. And now she's gone, and I love her." It took a little time to put together the pieces. It was the common story of a man returned from a prisoner-of-war camp to find his young wife, newly married when he left, had been unfaithful to him. "Try to understand and forgive," Hugh had told him.

"Prison camp was ghastly; but at least it had comradeship. Try to understand the long-drawn-out loneliness, and anxiety, the emotional tension of the "blitz" at home, the longing for protection and affection, of a highly strung girl with all her deepest instincts but recently awakened and brought to the surface. Be thankful that it is you she wants to come back to, and start again with mutual trust and no recriminations." But "trust and no recriminations" was too much for human pride and wounded vanity, and so "I *wouldn't* listen. And now she's gone. I've been a fool." Nevertheless, that was one of the stories with a happy ending. "There's always hope," Hugh would say, "when a man (or a woman) admits to having been a fool! It's when one, or both, are quite certain all the fault is on the other side that one can do little to help."

viii

At the opposite extreme to those who thought Hugh Warner too orthodox about divorce were those who considered him too *un*orthodox about contraception. A certain type of mind has a habit of grouping all moral questions together and simply applying a "catholic" or "liberal" solution, according to preference. Hugh's question always was, "Is it true?" and he approached each problem on its own merits. His criterion in both these matters was the true "end" of marriage; and of the three causes for which matrimony is ordained, as set out in the Prayer Book, he judged that while the advocates of divorce threatened the first (which concerns not only the begetting but also the upbringing of children), the advocates of "abstinence only" threatened the second, and both alike would frustrate the third. His thoughtfully argued essay on the subject, when he was still young and thinking out his position, had won him an "alpha" in one of his ordination examination papers, and behind the student was the little boy on the boat who had watched the first of his mother's many breakdowns, as she brought home from Africa her four babies born in such swift succession. Parish visiting both in Bishopthorpe and Epsom, as well as marriage guidance counselling, had convinced him that the failure to find a satisfactory solution to this question was at the bottom of many a marital breakdown, and that much unnecessary moral and spiritual conflict was caused in the minds of those whose conscience told them they were doing right and whose Church told them they were doing wrong.

He was always careful to make it crystal clear that the Church of England had never committed itself to any official doctrine in this respect. When "Catholic tradition" was invoked he would point out that *Roman* Catholic tradition has been largely coloured by the preponderant celibate influence on moral theology; while the appeal to the Early Fathers on this subject was ludicrous, since not only could they not discuss *contraception* in its modern scientific sense, but they could not really comprehend *conception,* being ignorant of relevant and vital biological facts, such as the existence of the ovum. Nevertheless, he always respected genuine scruples, and in his lectures to theological colleges he was careful to put the differing points of view within the Church with his usual fairness and balance, as they had been originally set out, and subsequently summed up by himself, in *The Threshold of Marriage.* "I'm not there to make up their minds for them," he would say, "but to see that they take all the relevant matters into consideration before making them up themselves"; and this he endeavoured to do in the seventh of his sex education booklets, *The Christian View of Sex.*

He was perfectly aware of the possible abuses: and writing home in July 1951 from a conference in Brussels of the International Union of Family Organizations, at which he was one of the British team, he says: "The Belgians are very bothered about their falling birth-rate. One quarter of all married couples have no children, and one quarter have only one. So they have started a League of Large Families ('3 plus' children)—sponsored strongly by the R.C.'s—which gives a medal to the mother (I'm trying to get two medals for you), reduced travelling charges, reduced cost of household goods and so on. It is all a rather interesting warning of the lengths to which Family Planning can go when faced with selfishness." This of course applies equally to every method of planning, including those employed in a Catholic country like Belgium.

In June 1953 he again attended an International Congress at the Oecumenical Institute at Bossey in Switzerland, at which he read a paper on *The Theological Implications of Contraception*. From here came the last of his letters from abroad. It contains all the characteristic ingredients.

"If only you could have been sitting by me tonight when the sun went down! The mountains all light up with gold and everything becomes so silent, except for the falling water of the little fountain in the gardens.

"An American family—friends of some one at the conference—asked me to tea at their lovely house right on the lake. She is a poet and anthropologist! *He* is 'something on U.N.O.'—and they have two boys, 11 and 13. These two took me sailing in their boat—and it was heavenly in the gentle breeze coming down from the mountains. Only when we came in was I told that they—the two boys—had only tried sailing three times before!

"I celebrated for the four Anglicans this morning in the turret of the castle which has been rigged up as a tiny chapel. We about filled it! Mattins, according to the American Episcopalian use, was said at the main conference service at 10 a.m. I pictured you all going to church at eleven as we sang a German hymn.

"At the concluding meeting this afternoon early, the members decided they would ask that my 'speech' should be circulated by the officers of the World Council to all consultant Churches. It was pointed out that this would set a precedent —as an *individual* contributor was never so dealt with. But they said, 'Let's start a precedent!'

"Later I proposed that a resolution be sent asking the W.C.C. to tackle family matters in their study programme and at the 2nd Assembly which takes place in America next year. So far the W.C.C. has *entirely* neglected the family! Tomorrow morning, as I pass through Geneva, I am instructed by the Conference to table our resolution personally —with 3 other people—and hand it to Visser 't Hooft, the General Secretary of the W.C.C. So it looks as if we may get the subject of sex, marriage and the family planted fully in the theological study of the various churches for the first time."

Hugh's paper was subsequently published as an article in *Theology* (January 1954) and he waited for the usual outburst of criticism and indignation. It never came. Shortly afterwards when visiting one of the most Anglo-Catholic of theological colleges, at which he had sometimes wondered if he was *persona grata*, the Principal astonished him by remarking, as he sat next to him at supper, "I've been reading your article in *Theology*. Very interesting. What's more, I'm not at all sure that you may not be right." It seemed that

Hugh's temperate and good-humoured style of controversy had disarmed opponents. The arguments, of course, were not all his own. As so often on the Council it was others— such as Dr Sherwin Bailey in this instance—who did the extensive research and the original thinking, but it was Hugh who would seize upon the relevant and essential points and present their arguments cogently to the appropriate audience. Sometimes, in his eagerness to popularize the fruits of others' labour, he was apt to forget the source of his ideas. Or, rather, it would be fairer to say that he was less concerned to stop and ask "whether it were I or they", than to pose the ever-important question, "Is it true?" and if so to convince others of the truth.

ix

Among the most intractable personal problems that caused increasing concern to Hugh Warner during the last years of his life was that of the male invert. Particularly he felt the unfairness of the distinction between men and women in this respect. Injustice always pained him; and he considered the harsh treatment meted out by society to those against whom the dice was already heavily loaded was out of proportion to the tolerant judgement of those whose sins left far more wreckage behind, creating the evils of V.D. and prostitution, or bequeathing to the community a harvest of unwanted babies, unmarried mothers, ruined marriages, divided homes and "problem" children, and all the troubles that constitute the perennial material of moral welfare work. It was a clear case of mankind's readiness to "Compound for sins they feel inclined to, By damning those they have no mind to". He knew from many personal confidences what the invert suffered from lack of ordinary decent friendships, as well as how difficult the present state of the law made it to offer such friendship, for fear of misunderstanding and blackmail, thus throwing such people back for necessary human affection on to the company of their own kind, with foreseeable results. More than one suicide known to him intensified his concern, while his dealings with schools convinced him of the necessity for sympathetic understanding and enlightened education (such as he himself endeavoured to give), rather than violent punishments and sometimes tragic expulsions as a solution to the problem.

Dr Sherwin Bailey, who had joined the Moral Welfare Council staff as lecturer shortly after Hugh became Education Secretary, had for some time been concerned with the whole subject of homosexuality, and together they had collected a small group of clergy, doctors, psychiatrists and others to study the question. When in 1953 certain *causes célèbres* brought the whole matter into sudden undue prominence in the Press, this committee decided that it was the time to publish their findings, as far as they had gone, and were faced with the choice of publishing their report themselves, or asking the Church of England Moral Welfare Council to do so. Urgent as Hugh felt the matter to be, this time he did not "rush" the Council. All members of the group felt the urgency, and were equally anxious for the Church's voice to be heard amongst the uproar. At the same time, it was obviously essential to make no false step through over-hasty drafting. It must, for instance, be made clear to all concerned that to demand justice for the invert was not to condone sin; and that in certain matters the Church would support an even stricter law—in making women, for instance, amenable as well as men to punishment for corrupting the young, and in penalties for assault, violence, offences to public decency, and soliciting. But the point must also be

driven home that in taking cognizance of the private behaviour of adults in this single instance the law not only
went beyond its normal boundaries, but aggravated the
problem both by the effect of its usual punishment (a prison
sentence) and by increasing the incidence of blackmail. Together with Dr Bailey Hugh wrote and rewrote the report,
submitting it and altering it again and again, explaining
and patiently endeavouring to carry with them the more
cautious members of the Council, until they had the full
weight of opinion behind the draft. It was probably the best
bit of true committee work that Hugh ever did.

The report was published in 1954 by the Council as an
interim report for private circulation, but a copy was sent to
every member of Parliament before the debates on the subject in both Houses. In the House of Lords there was some
adverse criticism, and one peer was outraged by the statement that "as a social problem it is not as a rule so far-
reaching and devastating in its third-party consequences as
ordinary pre-marital or extra-marital sexual relations". But
on the whole there was much honest appreciation of the fact
that the complexity of the problem had been very superfici-
ally understood hitherto. The distinction between sin and
temptation, between action and proclivity, between physical
behaviour and psychological condition had never occurred
to the ordinary member of society, who did not even know
the difference between inversion and perversion, and simply
assumed that to be a "homosexual" was in itself a crime.
In April 1954 the Government appointed the Wolfenden
Committee to look into existing laws relating to homosexual
offences. For Hugh it was a matter of triumphant pride that
for once the Church had, as he put it, "got in first". He had
always urged that Christians should be ahead of public
opinion, anticipating and thinking out problems *before* they

became subjects of popular discussion. "At last!" he exclaimed. "It's what I've wanted all my life—the Church ready to give a lead at the right moment."

x

Before this chapter ends there is a kind of interlude; one might call it the Indian Summer of a Parish Priest. "Now I'm going to see things from a layman's point of view," said the ex-Vicar of Epsom when he moved to Dorking. Apart from assisting at early celebrations and reading the lessons at evensong, he had asked the vicar not to expect any Sunday duty of him, and above all not to ask him to preach, since he was lecturing all the week. For three years he sat in his pew with the family every Sunday morning, enjoying the experience of being "congregation". At festivals he took one of the Communion services, and one Whitsuntide found him back in Scout circles, celebrating in the open air (and a downpour of rain) for a large Rover rally on Ranmore Common. But in 1953, partly for financial reasons, he decided to put his name on the supply list for "guinea-pig" duty in the diocese, and from time to time he relieved priests on holiday in the several villages around Dorking. He found that, though it meant a heavier Sunday, it was a joy to be back in the priest's stall again, and when in 1954 the little parish of Leigh near Reigate fell vacant, and he was asked if he would take charge of its services during the interval between incumbencies, he was glad to do so. He took the younger children in the car with him on Sundays, and they came to look on the little church as "Daddy's", and decided they would live in Leigh when he retired.

This subject often came up at home now, for the sands of his five-years' appointment were running out, and there was interested speculation as to what was to follow. Would he consent to go on for a further term if asked, or was five years of such work as much as anyone could bear to do? Was he longing to get back to parish life; and, if so, would it be a big one again or would he retire to Friday Street, his favourite beauty spot? His only comment as a rule on these frivolous family discussions was "No. I don't think I could tackle a big parish again. I've shot my bolt." A curious remark from an energetic man who was still under fifty. But what about the Epsom lady's "step to a bishopric"? If Hugh had ever been interested in such an ambition ("Oh dear no! I should have to make appointments"), he would have met with little domestic encouragement. The prospect involved too many new carpets and curtains; and there was a family joke that only one See would ever be considered—Hereford, because of its proximity to the Welsh border and the Wye Valley!

On Good Friday 1954 he was invited by the Dean of Windsor to take the Three Hours' Service in St George's Chapel. He had often tried in Epsom to make this less of a one-man virtuoso performance and more of a corporate meditation. Sometimes he simply read the whole story of the Passion, asking the congregation to sit and meditate after each section while the organist played an appropriate Bach chorale, followed by silence. Once he conducted the liturgical sequence of Mattins, Litany, Ante-Communion, and Evensong, with addresses only at the normal places. The Psalms, Lessons and Gospel for the day, he said, were of greater devotional value than any comment he could make. At Windsor he necessarily conformed to the more usual custom, with meditations on the Seven Words from the Cross. The Queen was abroad on her Australian tour, but the Queen Mother and the Princess Margaret were present. Hugh was no more nervous than he had been when, as a young man, he preached in front of an Archbishop. It was not, he remarked characteristically, the exalted personages who worried him, but the congregation, who seemed unable to relax! "They were so conscious of the presence of Royalty", while he was concerned, as ever, to make them conscious of the presence of God. "My dear Hugh—if I may make so bold", so wrote the Dean on Easter Sunday, "I am more than grateful, and all who sat under you, including the Queen and the Princess—and when my family tell me something of what you gave them and of how you gave it I am thoroughly happy."

So, too, were his little flock at Leigh, one of whom, writing after his death, used much the same phrase. "Only a year ago Canon Warner was giving us so much help by the personality he was—quite apart from all he gave us during the services. He and his family became part of us in those days—and that was something quite other than the number of Sundays he visited us. We valued it greatly, little knowing at the time how much too much he was giving to all." He was indeed nearly spent; but there was a new note of inspiration in his sermons. Preaching on the text, "Behold what manner of love the Father has shown us, that we should be called the Sons of God", as he compared the recognizable joy of a Christian to the glow of pride with which a young mother wheeling out her baby, or a young service man walking out in his uniform, proclaim to all around their new and exciting status, his own face seemed to glow with the radiance of a true son of God. His last sermon at Leigh—the last he ever preached—was on the words of Isaiah : *The spirit of the Lord is upon me . . . to proclaim to those that mourn in Zion . . . beauty for ashes, the oil of joy for mourning, a garment of praise for the spirit of heaviness."* "I have been looking up the text of his last sermon," wrote the churchwarden afterwards. "It was Isaiah 60. How well I remember that sermon! . . . and indeed the whole Evensong."

xi

Could we have had some respite from that race
We should regret now fewer things undone.

Hugh had little cause to regret things left undone at the Moral Welfare office. It was extraordinary, as Miss Steel remarked the week he went to hospital, how his every plan and project had been finished just in time : his contribution to the contraception argument published; the interim report on homosexuality in circulation; his latest pamphlets just through the Press; his last book on *Divorce and Remarriage* in the hands of the printers. All that remained was to tackle his lecturing engagements for the coming year, and those no one man could possibly have fulfilled in any case. He had hardly left himself time to travel from one to another, and they had to be divided up between half a dozen people. His illness in fact accelerated the task that had already begun, as the Council's Report the following year pointed out—the task of thinking out priorities and finding ways of devolving the work which had grown round the central staff.

The letters that came to the office in reply to the cancelling of Hugh's engagements, before people realized the nature of his illness, showed how the pressure of work in his case had come about. "I hope," came from one University College, "that your search for another speaker will be successful. Canon Warner was particularly acceptable because he approached the topic as someone who was prepared to speak the language of ordinary people, and not, as many parsons do, wave a holy but rather ignorant finger at the rest of mankind. If you cannot get someone who really satisfies Canon Warner as his substitute, please do not hesitate to say so. I would sooner postpone the conference than have the topic treated in a less satisfactory manner." And so said many others. In vain had Gilbert Russell warned at the outset of these five years, "Try to impress upon Hugh that his main job is not to be lecturing," since theological colleges, clergy schools, moral welfare associations and conferences all over the country would have him as lecturer and no substitute. His engagement lists for the past two years had revealed the ever-quickening pace, the ever-increasing area covered. The Public Morality Council summed it up in the first letter he received when his illness became known.

4 *Oct.* 54.

Dear Canon Warner,

It came as a real blow to the Executive Committee at its meeting on Thursday last to learn of the sudden illness which has overtaken you and laid you aside for the present.

We who have the best of all reasons for our belief, know that you have spent yourself in the heroic and monumental labours you have somehow accomplished, and although we are, as the hymn puts it, "lost in wonder, love and praise" at all you have done, the burden it has placed upon you must have been beyond human endurance.

We can only hope and pray that you may now be upheld by the prayers and affection of your countless colleagues, amongst whom there are many in this Council, and that you may be restored both to us and the work you love, as soon as is possible, without taking any risk to your health again.

Writing with difficulty, Hugh re-addressed the letter and sent it to his mother to comfort her.

PART III
TESTING

TESTING

Mephist: His faith is great; I cannot touch his soul,
But what I can afflict his body with
I will attempt; which is but little worth.

Marlowe—*Dr Faustus*

i

"IT may well be," wrote Bishop Hamilton, the Dean of Windsor, in the *Moral Welfare Quarterly* after Hugh's death, "that the best work Hugh ever did was achieved during the long, weary months of crippling sickness and pain which he faced without dismay or bitterness right through to the end, which is more truly the beginning." To allow pain or reticence to shroud those months in silence would be to falsify the story of Hugh's vocation; for surely this was its climax and its testing.

Had the gathering pace of those last breathless years accelerated the end? That, of course, was the common view. But those most close to Hugh were conscious of a different impression. It was rather as if he were pressing on because the time was short. There is no need to dwell on the increasing fatigue, the sleeplessness, the headaches and neuralgia, the diminished power of recuperation after colds and other disorders. Hugh did not dwell on them, nor on any of his troubles. When the specialist, puzzled by the persistence of his eczema so long after his Epsom illness, asked him if he was worrying about anything, Hugh, with all the anxieties of a large and growing family, and with a hundred people's problems on his heart, replied, "Worrying? I've

187

nothing to worry about. I'm a very *happy* man." "I think," he had once written from Westcott House, "it's that word 'worry' that's wrong."

His cheerfulness, enthusiasm and inherent capacity for forgetting himself in the demands of others, concealed from both his family and his colleagues how ill he was often feeling. Any set-back he simply treated as a case of *reculer pour mieux sauter,* and he generally came back from a few days in bed with a fresh bunch of "plans". On his holiday in Bangor, in the August of 1954, he was clearly unequal to any exertion, and refused an invitation to preach in the Cathedral, but he willingly attended a meeting of the local Moral Welfare Council, who sought his advice and guidance; and from Snowdonia he sent a picture post-card to a young man dying in Dorking. "All the beauty of Psalm 121," he wrote on the back, "is caught up in these lovely hills—a language which speaks what can never go into human speech. I have been thinking so much about you. Have no fears or anxieties. My prayers for the peace of God."

Returning home from Wales the car passed the scene of a serious accident, and the youngest of the party was badly shaken. Several evenings later, lying wakeful in bed, she asked her father, "Daddy, why do you think God *let* us see such a dreadful thing?" "I think," said Hugh, "that perhaps He wanted us to have a talk about death." It was a talk she was to remember and treasure afterwards.

Sunday, 19 September, was Hugh's Silver Wedding Day. He went to church with the family, walking slowly and stumblingly with a stick, and stood to sing the first hymn, "O God of Jacob," which had been the processional hymn at his wedding. But after the psalms he could not stand any more. "It was then," said someone in the congregation, "that I knew how ill he must be. To see him, of all people, *sit* for the Te Deum." Nevertheless, he continued visiting the office all that week, while he waited for an appointment with a nerve specialist whom Dr Eustace Chesser (with whom he was engaged in a piece of research work) had insisted on his consulting.

It was on Monday, 27 September (Michaelmastide again), that Hugh went to Guildford to keep the appointment. He returned at tea-time saying calmly that the specialist had tried several tests and X-rays and wanted him to go into hospital "for observation". While waiting for the X-ray results he had gone into a Guildford church and spent what he described as the worst hour in his life. "I asked God to forgive me," he said, "for being such a fool, running about all over the country like this and not thinking of you and the family." Fool? Perhaps, for no single mortal can indefinitely shoulder every burden and respond to all demands. Yet it is a foolishness one could not wish away without wishing that Hugh Warner had not been the man he was— "One who has not spared himself, and has radiated the Divine Love among us." What passed between him and God in that hour in church one cannot know; one can but remember the counsel he had always given others in times of fear and stress: "Look the worst that can possibly happen in the face, and then trust God to see you through."

Calmly now he sat down at his study desk, saying that he had some writing he must do; and half an hour later he joined the family at the tea-table. It was the last meal he would have with them. Feeling the hand that held his fork begin to shake violently, he stumbled quickly from the room so that the children should not be distressed, and was with difficulty helped upstairs to bed. Within a few days his left side was completely paralysed.

"I suppose you have been in the study looking up the difference between a cyst and a tumour in the medical dictionary?" he said quietly that evening. "Indeed I haven't! What *is* the difference?" Carefully he explained. "So you see, if it's just a cyst, it's quite a quick business"; and he added, "You'll get a lot of sympathy. Anything to do with the brain always *sounds* so much worse; but it is only a part of the body after all."

On 12 October he was taken to the National Hospital for Nervous Diseases in Queen Square. With his papers in the study was found a large envelope inscribed simply "My affairs". Its contents were what he had written in that half-hour before tea the day he returned from Guildford. It was headed, "An Exercise in Common Sense," and it set out with careful precision, though in erratic handwriting, advice about the house, the children's education, the insurance policies, ending with "Funeral: service at Epsom", and the telephone number of the Epsom undertakers. (How often he had dealt with those practical details for his parishioners.) The envelope had been re-opened and he had added in a postscript, "If you peep at this before you should, remember this is only an exercise in common sense. I'm feeling in fine fettle; and there's Hereford ahead! Bless you, my darling."

The doctor reported the result of the National Hospital's investigations. "It was agreed that you should be told the truth—but not Canon Warner." "But do you really think, Doctor, that he doesn't know? A man with his experience of parish and hospital visiting?" "Oh no! One never thinks these things happen to oneself. A man who spots it at once in anyone else never suspects it in himself though it sticks out a mile." It was Plato's "medical lie", to comfort the relations. But Hugh's old parishioners in Epsom professed later that what had proved a far greater comfort and inspiration was to realize that he *had* known, and had faced it as courageously as he had faced a very different conflict many years before. Was it in those wartime years, or was it but recently, that he had made one of the rare marks in his Office book against the verse of a psalm? "Nevertheless though I am sometime afraid, yet put I my trust in Thee."

On the morning of his operation, as he lay waiting outside the operating theatre, he whispered, ". . . *work together for good*"; and afterwards, when asked if it had seemed a terribly long time waiting for them to begin, he answered, "Just long enough for me to say the Te Deum."

"We are sending you to St Thomas's Hospital for a few weeks' treatment," the surgeon told him after the operation, "and we want you to cancel your engagements for six months." Hugh looked at him thoughtfully. "Six months," he said slowly. It was not to be a "quick business". But his first thought was for his fellow-patients, still waiting their turn. "I want you," he said to me, "to go straight down to the other ward and tell them from me that it's not nearly as bad as it is made out."

ii

During the last year Hugh had begun, but not finished, a series of addresses, mainly on the theme of Spiritual Healing, intended for the B.B.C. *Lift up Your Hearts* programme, one of which had ended:

"Sickness is never a thing to give in to. We are called to do something about it; rather, to conquer its domination over us by accepting its disciplines creatively, with no self-pity, and to look forward with high hope to restoration of spiritual (and maybe physical) health."

"Accepting its disciplines creatively. . . ." Throughout the painful period of treatment at St Thomas's Hospital he had one recurring idea—to help the doctors; somehow to make use of this experience so that others might benefit. "It's the wrong people," he would say, "who write the books and do the research on pain. It's the people who suffer it who *know*. I must write a book about it." It was the same Hugh Warner who had become the expert on one concern after another.

"No self-pity." But he missed his work, "the finest bit of work I've ever been associated with", as he said to Miss Steel when she brought him news of how it was going. And suddenly one day he asked, "How's the Church of England?" "Still there, dear! Missing you a bit, I dare say." "I miss it," he said sadly, "I miss working for it." "You *are* working for it," we told him. His ministry was not over yet. Many months later the chaplain at the National Hospital wrote of him, "Although these months of illness have debarred him from the exercise of his ministry, he has in a sense been ministering to us all the time. It is always a wonderful thing when a devoted priest comes here and shows how to bear pain, privation and suffering."

Daily the drastic treatment brought him lower and left him weaker; but daily, too, the letters poured in by the score, bringing news of groups and individuals praying, and of congregations remembering him at many an altar. ("What a lot one learns in illness," he said, "of the meaning of the Mystical Body.") Perhaps the most moving was from the headmistress of a private school in Epsom, who wrote, "Jill, Jeremy and Christine informed me that they are praying for Canon Warner 'at night and lots of other times', and at lunch-time today I was astonished to hear their 'table' add, after grace, 'and please make Hugh Warner well again'— just like that. Children never cease to amaze and touch me. There was a terrific silence after that for some time." Hugh had always been loved by children, but it was over four years now since he had left these in Epsom.

It was given to him also just at this crucial time to know some of the harvest of his labours. "If he is well enough," wrote a young couple in difficulties with in-laws, "*please* let him know that his advice is working out in the most miraculous way. There have been all the snags and set-backs he warned us of, but thanks to his wise advice, the relationship is sorting itself out and the bitterness has gone. Tell him we are just two more grateful friends who thank God for his wonderful understanding of human problems and his help in applying the Christian answer." Out of the blue (for the writer did not know that Hugh was ill, or even that he had left Epsom) came a letter from one of the "pagans" whose wedding he had taken some years before. "Dear Canon Warner," he wrote, "I have never forgotten the promise I made to you four years ago when I was married in your church, that I would come to a decision regarding my entry into the Church. At last I can tell you that I have been baptized and confirmed into the Church of England. Today I attended my first Communion Service."

The last letter to be read to him while he could still understand came from his old Luton vicar, Jack Woodhouse, then Bishop of Thetford, himself partially paralysed after a stroke, and shortly to precede Hugh into the life to come.

"I can picture," he wrote, "a little of what the feeling of utter dependence you must be facing is. It brings home to you, as no other way can, how much we depend on those around us and also on God Himself. 'What have I that I did not receive?' You will find how much kindness and goodness surrounds us. It is, after all, a reflection of the love of God. Eighteen months ago I had to realize that I had come to the end of my ministry, and to offer it back to Our Lord who first commissioned me, for what it was worth, and I think I realized that success or failure did not count nearly so much as I thought. 'Rejoice not that the devils are subject unto you, but that your names are written in heaven.' "

On 21 November, "Stir-up Sunday", the Bishop of St Albans (Hugh's chairman on the Moral Welfare Council) came to give him the sacrament of Holy Unction. It was a day of light in the midst of the gathering black-out, for Hugh, who had been somnolent and unresponsive all the week, was fully conscious of what was going on and deeply moved by it. "This is the biggest thing that has ever happened to me," he said with tears in his eyes. The following week he had forgotten many things, but when asked, "Do you remember Michael St Albans coming to anoint you?" he replied simply, "Of course. One doesn't forget a thing like *that*." Prayer and Communion, the familiar means of grace, were too difficult when the mind could not concentrate nor the paralysed throat swallow easily; but this one sacrament could pierce the barrier of sickness with the objective reassurance of the love of God, and it brought the help needed to face the further descent into darkness.

On the last day of his treatment, when told that it was finished and asked if he was not glad it was over, he gasped, "Oh yes, I've been so afraid it would all be wasted. You see," he explained, speaking slowly and with difficulty, "I've been trying to garner—every bit of experience—to help the doctors." After that he steadily descended into a deep coma, and lay between life and death for a fortnight. "It's the courage of a jet pilot," said a friend, "reporting to base while he crashes."

iii

Two days before Christmas Hugh recovered consciousness.

For the children at home, as he would have wished, it was a joyful Christmas, but to those near him it was clear that it was not the whole Hugh that had come back. When in the new year he returned to the National Hospital it was in much distress of body and confusion of mind. In the midst of his confusion, however, he was very clear about his work, and was cheered when the Chaplain brought him the *Church Times'* review of his book, *Divorce and Remarriage*. "I have *so* prayed," he said earnestly, "that it might help to turn the tide."

He was clear, too, about his faith. On a day when he was very restless in mind and body the annual News Letter from Westcott House arrived. He scarcely seemed to listen as it was read to him, until one sentence arrested his attention. "Surely faith in Christ is, of its very being, a call to *insecurity* at every level except that of the ultimate conviction of His eternal presence and victory. . . . Unless we preach Christ who uproots before He fulfils all things, we are preaching not Christ but a human construction." "Read that again," said Hugh suddenly at the last sentence, and when it had been repeated, "That's very well put—*very* well put!" So had he written himself, in his own Westcott House days, of all false securities, traditionalist or fundamentalist, "We must ride loose, I'm certain." Christ's eternal presence and victory was the sure foundation of all his sermons.

He was being given physiotherapy for the paralysis, but the demand on the injured brain was too great; and though the other patients remarked on the sense of humour which still flashed out in the midst of his confusion, life in a general ward was clearly a strain on the impaired nervous system. Yet through all the mental and physical distress there spoke the old Hugh Warner. "When you speak at your next meeting," he said, "you must speak about Christian joy." "And what shall I say about it?" "Tell them that Christian joy doesn't mean enjoying yourself, but enjoying God: and that's important—*very* important, because nothing can take it from you, even in times of desolation."

"He was a wonderful man, even when he was so very ill," a nurse wrote afterwards. "Such illnesses often change people, but it was not so in his case, because his own self, his soul, perhaps, never failed to shine through." "I think I rarely met a patient," wrote another one, "who so radiated the love of God."

iv

A fortnight before Easter 1955 Hugh was moved to St Luke's Hostel, the Clergy Nursing Home in Fitzroy Square, where those he loved, who understood the inner logic of his mind, could come often to be with him. "Remember," he had said, when first foreseeing what would come, "the brain is only a part of the body after all." Brain and body were both impaired, but the spirit was still recognizable, even as familiar music, distorted by a broken instrument, is recognizable to those who know the tune.

There was a day when he talked of everything and everybody as Japanese. "But why are we all Japanese today, Hugh?" He looked surprised. "Haven't we just finished a war with Japan?" "Well—yes, some time ago." "And we won?" "Oh yes, we won." "Well, then, I think we should be trying to feel what it's like to be Japanese." "Oh, but *isn't* that in character!" exclaimed an Epsom friend, coming in just then. All the old pages in the Gazette . . . "We should be trying to feel what it's like" to be a Jewish refugee, an unemployed man, an unmarried mother, a displaced person. "Somebody," the *New Statesman* had written, reviewing the Interim Report on Homosexuality, "somebody on this

Committee has really tried to imagine what it feels like to be an invert."

This imaginative sympathy was carried to its logical conclusion in that darkest phase of his illness, in which he imagined himself guilty of a different crime every day, and was anxious to confess every kind of heinous sin. To those who knew the scope of his work in the last few years, and the many wicked, weak and tempted who had given him their confidence, this "time of desolation" showed the true meaning of his work. It seemed a significant insight when a man, serving a long term for theft, wrote at this time from prison to ask after "the Canon": "Life sometimes gives us much to bear, and often it falls upon those we feel should never have the weight. But I do believe a good man can take on himself the weakness of others. To many who knew him he will always be the spirit of Charity." At the heart of Hugh's work for Moral Welfare there was indeed that charity which the late Charles Williams taught us to know as the mystery of exchange; and this was its final test.

The mental suffering passed. He was growing weaker in body, and speech was becoming harder. When it came it was, some would say, only reflex action. But it is that which reveals the dominant notes in a man's life, and from time to time the chords vibrated to the right touch. When the familiar words were read to him, "This is a true saying and worthy of all men to be received, that Christ Jesus came into the world to save sinners," he murmured, "A true saying! Isn't that *good* to remember?" And one was reminded of how as a young priest, memorizing the Comfortable Words, he had said, "I can always remember which it is that 'Paul saith'; this is a *true* saying." Paul always asks, "Is it true?"

One day, not long before the end, one came in with the

news that the Church Bookshop had devoted its window, and S.P.C.K. was also giving prominence, to the theme nearest his heart, the Christian view of marriage, sex and the family. He paid no heed. Once again he had passed his goal without noticing it and was set for further horizons.

There were some friends whose faith still clung to nearer horizons, and who, remembering Hugh's own belief in spiritual healing, persistently prayed for recovery in this world. But this was a time, Hugh would have told them, to look forward and not back. The Slough of Despond and the Hill Difficulty were behind him now; there is no looking back when the Celestial Mountains are in sight. A letter from the Bishop of St Albans at this time put things in perspective.

"The agony of these months is better looked upon as travail. With your discernment I know you'll be thinking of the kernel within the shrinking husk, realizing that Hugh is growing in spiritual stature all these days and resting in the Lord now before campaigning in Paradise. Just what he'll be given to do there who can say, but that he will be even more used than he has ever been in this life (and that says something) I am quite certain.

"I often think we over-emphasize the importance of life here in relation to life in the world to come. We want our best men to remain here and we are shaken when a William Temple is suddenly taken from us, but are we not right to expect that each of us will exercise a fuller ministry according to our gifts, when we have passed through the gate of death? What sort of ministry it will be I have no idea, except that it will be a better expression of our love for God and each other."

Hugh had fulfilled his ministry for Moral Welfare to the day. 30 June found him very weak, and as he settled peacefully to sleep the night-sister said, "He will probably go into a coma now and slip quietly away." But Hugh would meet death, like life, with his eyes open. Early the next morning he was awake, and all that Friday he lay motionless, watching through half-closed eyes and, it seemed, waiting.

He had had his last Communion some time before. It had been difficult, for he could not swallow and no one knew what he understood. But now he seemed to listen as, sitting by his bed, I read the familiar things, the 23rd Psalm and the 103rd, and talked of those who had gone ahead of him.

At mid-day Cyril came and said the Commendatory Prayers. But it was not until the evening, when his two elder sons had come, that he was ready to go. His eyes were wide open and he was breathing hard and heavily. As every night for the last nine months, I said his favourite Compline prayer: "Be present, most merciful Father, and protect us through the silent hours of this night; so that we who are wearied by the changes and chances of this fleeting world, may repose on Thy eternal changelessness." There was silence. The heavy breathing waited, as he closed his eyes and listened. Then, as it began again, the four of us repeated the final words of commendation:

Go forth upon Thy Journey from this world, O Christian soul,
In the name of God the Father Almighty who created thee,
In the name of Jesus Christ who suffered for thee,
In the name of the Holy Ghost who strengtheneth thee,
In Communion with the blessed Saints, and aided by Angels and Archangels, and all the armies of the heavenly host,
May thy portion this day be in peace, and thy dwelling in the Heavenly Jerusalem. Amen.

EPILOGUE

"Then I heard that all the bells in the city rang again for joy, and that it was said unto them, Enter ye into the joy of your Lord."

Bunyan: *Pilgrim's Progress*

Hugh Warner's last service sounded his most characteristic note, the note of Christian joy. When he had bidden farewell to Epsom, in September 1950, St Martin's congregation could not remember a wetter Harvest, "inside the Church, or out!" When, on 6 July 1955, his body was brought back to rest before the altar, the sun shone brilliantly and no tears marred the thanksgiving.

The church, ablaze with lilies and delphiniums, pulsing with the calm steadfast beat of the Bach voluntary, reflected that blend of truth and beauty which he had ever brought into the worship of God. The hymns, "O Jesus, I have promised", "O love that will not let me go", "Light's abode, celestial Salem", told of a vocation fulfilled, a life surrendered, and pain transcended. The lessons, from his much-loved 1928 service, spoke of the light affliction that worketh a more exceeding weight of glory, when the former things shall have passed away. There was no need of sermon. "What to some may have seemed a theory was here demonstrated as a fact"[1] (Hugh's authentic message seemed to sound through the service), "Death is for the Christian a gateway, not a cul-de-sac. The fellowship of those who find their unity in the love of God extends beyond the grave."

After the procession of choirs from three Epsom churches,

[1] Christian Youth Leadership (see page 113).

the robed clergy, and the Diocesan Bishop in cope and mitre, some noticed a young girl, hatless and stockingless, in cotton summer frock, enter with her shopping basket and slip into a pew to pray, "for all the world as if she had just dropped in to see a friend off".

The simple note; and also the dramatic, for unexpectedly the ringers had freed their bells, which all the previous Sunday had been muffled. As Hugh's body was carried from the crowded church they broke into a joyous peal, and the family, glancing upwards startled, beheld the flag, at half-mast when they entered, now floating serenely from the mast-head. "Rejoice," Hugh's old vicar had written, shortly before his own death, "that your names are written in heaven." And now the text of Hugh's own sermon, ". . . that we should be called the sons of God", seemed to be caught up and counterpointed by the Epistle for the week. In the words of one, writing long afterwards, "I remember being tremendously certain, in the week Hugh died, of the application of the Epistle for Trinity IV to his passing; particularly as it appears in J. B. Phillips' translation—'The whole creation is on tiptoe to see the wonderful sight of the sons of God coming into their own . . . ' and so on, as the words rush on to the end of that passage. Over the whole thought is that triumphant peal of bells at St Martin's, as he passed out through the west door. But that is wrong—he was *everywhere* that day in church."

In the cemetery, close to a little row of war-time graves, Cyril committed his brother's body to the earth; while in the church the choir was singing "Blessed are the dead that die in the Lord. Even so, saith the Spirit, for they rest from their labours." "Do you notice," one wrote, "that the anthem does not finish the verse (Rev. 14. 15)? But I finished it in my heart, praying that we all might be a little worthier for those 'works' of Hugh's given us for twelve years here. 'And their works do follow them.'" Afterwards, the Church Council chose these words for the plaque which commemorates him in the sanctuary.

In Bishopthorpe, too, his old parishioners remembered, holding a Memorial Service on the same day. A week later the Moral Welfare Council gave thanks for his "works" in a Memorial Service held in St Martin-in-the-Fields. All his colleagues, as well as the typists in the office, had contributed their suggestions to the suffrages.

Thanks be unto Thee, O Lord, for the work and witness of Thy servant whom we honour before Thee:

For his total consecration to God;

For his thoughtfulness for others and the breadth of his sympathies; for his generous giving of himself and his tireless efforts to help those in difficulty;

For his home and family life;

For his service to the Church in interpreting the Christion teaching on marriage and personal relation; for his fight to protect young people from the power of evil suggestion; for his watchfulness of the printed word and the vigour of his pen in attacking false standards;

For his work as a teacher of the clergy and laity;

For his faithful ministry as a parish priest, and as a pioneer in Church youth work;

For his serenity, fortitude and Christian witness during his long illness.

The letters poured in—many have been quoted in the course of this book—striking three predominant notes: the unique value of his work for the Church ("There is no one else could have done what he did"); his care for people ("I think he was the *kindest* man I ever met"; "I feel I have lost the best friend I ever had"); and the deep impression left even, it might be, by but a single encounter, of a serene and radiant Christian faith ("*He* won't be forgotten easily," a simple woman put it quaintly, "not with that glorious smile"). Over four hundred such letters were received at home, besides many more sent to Church House with contributions, large and small, to his Memorial Fund, from Moral Welfare Associations all over the country, from Church Societies (Anglican, Free Church and Roman Catholic), from Public Bodies, and from countless individuals who wrote with heartfelt gratitude of what Hugh Warner's life-work, "showing people how to love each other", had meant to them personally.

The obituary notices concentrated on his Youth work, on Marriage Guidance, or on Moral Welfare according to the main interest of the organ concerned; but Dr Mervyn Haigh, ex-Bishop of Winchester, who had been Vice-Principal of Knutsford in Hugh's student days, saw the picture as a whole.

"Had Knutsford done nothing else," he wrote in the Knutsford Fellowship Paper, "than provide a means whereby Hugh Warner was assisted in putting his sense of vocation to the test and in beginning to equip himself for its discharge, it would have done no small service to Church and State; and not often is the death of a priest in the Church of England quite as widely and deeply mourned as was his. . . . From the very beginning of his ministry . . . he was not only greatly beloved, nor yet only an effective influence for good in the lives of great numbers of his parishioners, but was enabled to bring many individuals into Christian discipleship and active membership of the Church. Pastor through and through, he became an expert in the field of personal relationships, especially between the sexes, and it was not surprising that the Church of England Moral Welfare Council should in the end have claimed his whole-time service.

"Those who knew Hugh will ever think of him as 'a burning and a shining light', not without its call and summons to themselves."

With such a verdict this book comes to an end. But not the story; for, as one letter put it, in a Pauline mixture of metaphors, "Many of the fruits of the foundations he has been laying are yet to evolve"; or as his Chairman on the Moral Welfare Council, the Bishop of St Albans, wrote on the day of his funeral: "You know that you are still a fellow-worker with Hugh, and both of you and all of us fellow-workers with God—who gave us Hugh to love and Himself in Hugh—so thanks be to GOD."